Obrunni!

Or

A Year in Ghana

Ian Schagen

Published by

Ian Schagen

40 Priestley Court

High Wycombe HP13 7WZ, UK

Using Kindle Direct Publishing

ISBN: 9798864839904

To Sandie

With thanks for her helpful comments and copy-editing skills

Contents

Map of Ghana

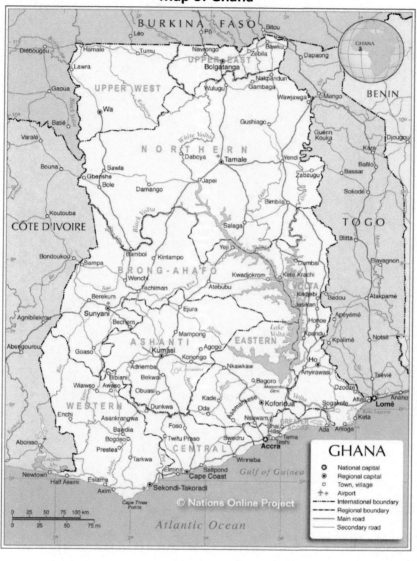

© Nations Online Project

Chapter 1: A Change of Plan

As we walked up the High Street in Putney, we were excited, slightly nervous, but pretty confident. Excited, because we were going to get the opportunity to do something we wanted to do – live and work in a developing country. Nervous, because we were going for our assessment day at VSO (Voluntary Services Overseas), and being assessed gives everyone nerves to some extent. Confident, because we had already had email correspondence with VSO, and they said we had just the skills and experience they needed.

Sandie and I had retired together in April 2008 from the National Foundation for Educational Research (NFER). She was a Principal Research Officer, in charge of managing a variety of research projects, and I was Head of Statistics, overseeing a team of statisticians analysing all kinds of educational data. On our retirement we went to work in New Zealand for almost two years, in Wellington, the capital. I worked for the Ministry of Education, and Sandie was at the New Zealand Council for Educational Research for a year, and then worked at the Ministry on a range of projects. Now we wanted to live and work in a developing country, and an application to VSO seemed the obvious choice.

We had applied from New Zealand, but were told VSO would not accept applications from overseas, so we had to wait until we got back to the UK at the end of July. We applied as soon as we got back, and were told "At this stage your skills and experience appear to match our current long-term volunteer role requirements and would therefore like to invite you to move on to the next stage of the application process and complete the full application form". So we both filled in the online forms, and eventually we received our invitations to go to the assessment day in Putney on 28th September 2010.

Now, as well as being a bit of an expert on the statistics of assessment, I have been through a number of assessments in my chequered career, including exams, job interviews, driving tests and a PhD viva. My rule has always been 'be yourself', and it has largely stood me in good stead – not on this occasion, as will become clear. The assessment day comprised group exercises, overseen by a guy with a clipboard, and individual interviews. At the end we felt we had acquitted ourselves reasonably well.

The next day we got the eagerly-awaited email from VSA – and to our great disappointment, we had both been rejected! The email said, among other things: "We do, of course, recognise that you have numerous professional skills and qualities. The Selectors' decision not to proceed was in no way meant to be a negative judgement of these. Rather, the placement requests that are now being generated by VSO partners require a balance of professional and personal qualities and our assessment process is designed to identify individuals who most nearly match these particular demands". In other words, we may have professional skills but our personal qualities are not what they were looking for.

Sandie had failed because of single comment which was taken the wrong way by the assessor, and which she tried to explain. But there is no appeal and no second chance from this assessment – one strike and you are out, however mistakenly.

Flattened and dejected, we tried to pick ourselves up and find a Plan B which would enable us to fulfil our dream of living and working in a developing country. We began surfing the net looking for other organisations that sponsored volunteers overseas. We found a number, but further research always led back to VSO – banned by them, banned by all. In desperation, we emailed all the contacts we could think of who might have a lead to a possible opening for us.

To stave off the gloom, we began making plans for a tour of South America in the new year. We threw ourselves into this, and the more we researched options the longer our itinerary got, growing from an initial three months to five months. We began to get excited at the prospect, and made enquiries about flight options.

Then suddenly we got a belated positive response from one of the contacts we had frantically emailed, Professor James Tooley of Newcastle University. I had known him briefly in my early days at NFER, before he went on to other things. Later I met him at a UN conference in London, and he commissioned us at NFER to analyse some data he had collected about the progress made by pupils in low-cost private schools and others in Hyderabad, India. After we had done the analysis we published a joint paper on the results[1].

James' main educational theory is that children in developing countries can often be better served by low-cost privately-run schools than by government schools, even if (or maybe because) the parents have to contribute a very small daily amount to their children's schooling. He has spent a lot of time and energy scouring the world for evidence to support this contention, and written a book ('The Beautiful Tree'[2]) and many papers to illustrate it.

As leftward-leaning aged hippies we tended to be doubtful of this theory, but the evidence from Hyderabad convinced us to at least keep open minds, and to accept that in some cases state-sponsored education in the third world might not be the panacea it is often sold as.

Unusually for an academic, James has bolstered his theories by investing in and setting up chains of such low-cost schools – a rare example of a professor who puts his money where his mouth is. Initially he set up schools in India, but he contacted us to say he had just launched a chain of schools in Ghana, and would we be interested in working with them?

Needless to say, we jumped at the chance, especially as he was offering us a three-bedroomed house to live in while we were there. We started to make plans that, once the 6-month tenancy on our flat was up in January, we would be off to Ghana. Things seemed to be back on track.

Because James spends a lot of time travelling around the world, he can be a hard man to pin down and communicate with, and we began to get a bit frustrated that we were not getting answers to all the practical questions we had – visas, insurance and so forth. Then, just before Christmas 2010, there was a heavy snowfall in England, and I managed to slip over and

---

[1] https://eric.ed.gov/?id=ED502371
[2] https://www.amazon.co.uk/Beautiful-Tree-Personal-Educating-Themselves/dp/1933995920

break my wrist. My arm being in plaster didn't necessarily mean an end to our plans, but it added to the complications.

In January 2011 we received an email from Ken Donkoh, CEO of Omega Schools Ghana, with details of the proposed accommodation. Our 3-bedroomed house had been transformed into a single room in the Omega office space! We responded at once and said it wasn't suitable, and eventually we got a reply saying they were not really ready for us, and would prefer to wait till later. So for the second time our hopes were dashed, and we seemed to be back to square one.

Having got our 5-month tour of South America pretty well organised, and then put on hold when we thought Ghana was going ahead, it came off the back burner again and had the heat turned up. In a flurry of emails and phone calls we booked all the flights we needed, and a flat to stay in when we got to Buenos Aires. In no time we had shelved one set of plans, dusted off another set, and were good to go.

Five months later, we came back to no permanent home in the UK, and uncertainty about whether the Ghana project was happening at all. Eventually we heard that a flat had been found for us, but there were still uncertainties around things like insurance, travel costs, and visas. In order to make progress we decided to fund our own travel and insurance for the three months up to the end of 2011, and see how it went from there. If we were unhappy, or they were unhappy with us, we would have had the experience and would walk away. Otherwise, we could continue on a more formal basis.

Our next challenge was to get visas. As we were volunteers, we did not need work visas, which made life slightly simpler, but not a lot. Two websites gave guidance on applying for visas, but they gave different advice. The official line seemed to be to fill in a downloaded form and take it to the Ghanaian embassy, with photos and so forth, so on the 15th September we caught an early train to London and headed over to the Ghanaian embassy. We had decided that I would go on my own to Ghana in the first place, and Sandie would come out later after our newest grandson was born, and she therefore had more time to get her visa by post.

On reaching the embassy, we discovered the system had changed! You now had to apply online and get an appointment for an interview, quite contrary to what the embassy website had said. I shot off down the road and found an internet café, where I filled in the online application and managed to get an appointment for 11.30 the same day. Back I went, and then sat in the crowded waiting room for two hours until I was seen and was able to hand over my application.

I returned to the embassy to collect my passport and visa on 20th September, but only had to wait half an hour this time. Back home, we heard that we had the go-ahead for me to go to Ghana on 28th September. I tried to book a direct British Airways flight to Accra, but the system refused to accept my credit card. Later on we discovered that this was standard with BA – they will not let anyone use credit cards for flights to or from Africa. Eventually I managed to book an indirect flight with KLM via Amsterdam, so it was all over bar the packing.

Obrunni!

Chapter 2: I Take the Plunge

Arrival

On 28th September I flew to Accra. Never having been to sub-Saharan Africa before, I was rather nervous about plunging into an unfamiliar region and culture. I was slightly heartened by a guidebook which said that Ghana was 'Africa light', and a good starting place for those who had never visited the continent before. By this it meant the country is economically and politically stable, with English as the official language and low levels of crime and corruption.

Our daughter Claire drove me to the airport, with Sandie and our grandson Charlie. It was an emotional parting, as since our marriage in 1970 we had never been apart for more than a few days. Sandie was going back with Claire to squeeze in a bedroom with Charlie and wait for the birth of our second grandson. Between us we were going to have some eventful and traumatic experiences over the next month before we joined up again.

It was a short hop to Amsterdam, and then quite a long time wandering round the enormous expanse of Schiphol airport to find the right gate for Accra. The flight itself was pleasant enough, and we landed at Accra at 8 pm. Then there was the queue for immigration, which was long and tedious, but eventually I emerged with my bags into the chaos of the terminal building. I was met by Ken Donkoh, the tall smiling CEO of Omega Schools, who led me out to his car for the drive to the area west of Accra where the schools are based.

I soon discovered that the traffic near the capital was horrendous, due to the major roadworks taking place all round the city, especially to the west. We seemed to sit for ages in long queues of cars, and I had no idea where I was or where we were going. Eventually we got clear, and then turned on to a steep dirt road where the car lurched and bumped about wildly. What was happening? Where was I? I clung on desperately and held on to the belief that Ken knew where he was going.

Finally we drew up outside a block of four flats, and Ken announced that this was my new home, upstairs on the first floor. We were greeted warmly by some of the neighbours, and carried the bags inside. I looked around blinking, and Ken showed me the kitchen and the few items of equipment there. Then he left, saying he would be back in the morning, and I was alone in my new home.

The flat had a large lounge and a dining room, as well as a spacious kitchen and two big bedrooms, and two bathrooms. There was plenty of room, but the flat was very sparsely furnished. There was a sofa and two chairs in the lounge, a table with chairs and a fridge in the dining room, one bed in the main bedroom, and a two-ring gas burner in the kitchen. The only

curtains in the bedroom were roughly draped over the window grills, and there was no bedding.

There was a water heater in the bathroom, but when I turned on the taps there was just a mere trickle and no hot water. I improvised some bedding, and lay down to sleep.

Our bedroom

First day

The road to Gbawe Top Base

In the morning I waited for someone to turn up and take me to the office. Over the next few days I gradually came to understand the local geography. The main coast road from Accra to the west passes to the south. There is a junction where a tarmacked side road leads off to the small town of Weija, passing through the village of Oblogo on the way. Oblogo lies at the foot of the hill on which our flat was perched, a location known as 'Gbawe Top Base'. From Oblogo a steep rutted dirt road leads up the hill and on towards Gbawe on the far side, and our flat was located up a series of tracks leading from the main dirt road. Taxis and other traffic regularly rattled and lurched up and down the hill, even though to my mind the track was only suitable for rugged four-wheel-drive vehicles.

About 9.30 Ken arrived, in order to show me the path down the hill to the office. The path was frankly quite steep and slippery to start with, and it ended up going through the rubbish tip. The Omega Schools office was on the top floor of their Oblogo school, a bleak

Oblogo School courtyard

and roughly-built structure with a central courtyard. I was greeted warmly, and shown into a desk in Andrew Ofosu-Dankyi's office (the head of teaching and learning). I connected to their wifi and sent an email to Sandie with updates on events so far.

A bit later, Ken announced he was free and we could go shopping. He drove me back to the main road, and along to the Shoprite supermarket, which is part of a South African chain and the only western-style supermarket in the area. I grabbed a trolley and began loading up with what I guessed might be needed. We then loaded it all into Ken's car and drove back, stopping to buy a multiway adaptor for the fridge and kettle, which would not plug into the existing sockets.

Electrical equipment in Ghana is imported from a variety of countries, with different types of plugs, so it is common to need a multiway adaptor in order to connect anything to the mains sockets, which are generally 3-

pin British style. However, the adaptors tend to come from China and are not always terribly reliable. We drove back to the flat and unloaded, and moved the fridge into the kitchen. Unfortunately, when we plugged the fridge and kettle into the adaptor, it blew up. Ken went off to get a new one, and I stayed behind.

After a while with no sign of him, I decided to walk back to the office by the 'road', partly to see how far it was. It was a longer but less steep route than the morning's, and took me past a number of dilapidated shacks on the bottom road selling various stuff. I also passed a lot of children coming out of school, who greeted me with 'Hey, Obrunni!' ('white man'), and I responded with 'Hey, black kids!', and there were smiles all round. I reached the school after 25 minutes and sat in Andrew's office for a bit, sending and reading emails. Then I packed up our laptop and headed back the same way, taking about 25 minutes again.

I waited there until Ken turned up with new adaptors, a gas canister, a clothes drying rack, food processor, iron, ironing board, mop, broom and bucket. I was able to make a cup of tea, get the fridge going, and we got the cooking rings working. After he'd gone I sorted out my clothes a little bit and did some stuff on the laptop. I tried to get the hot water system working, with no success, so at about 6 pm I had a shower in a trickle of cold water, which was not so bad given the ambient temperature.

Ghana is just north of the equator, so the temperature does not vary throughout the year and is usually about 30°C. The flat had no air conditioning, but the windows all opened and were covered with mesh to keep bugs out, and there were ceiling fans in each room. With these the temperature was not a serious problem and we never felt that we really needed air conditioning.

I was cooking myself some dinner when I experienced the first of many power cuts. This one lasted about an hour, but as we got used to them we realised that they varied greatly in duration. Sometimes they lasted for four hours, often from 6 pm to 10 pm, and we deduced that these were deliberate 'load shedding' due to insufficient capacity in the grid. At other times they were probably due to local equipment failures, and could go on for an indeterminate period – the longest we experienced was 48 hours.

Fortunately Ken had left me an emergency lamp, which charged itself from the mains when there was power and came on automatically when the power failed, so I was able to see to cook, eat and read while the mains were off. Unfortunately, when I tried to plug the emergency lamp back in, I managed to break its plug (see previous remarks about the low quality of electrical equipment). I now had an impressive list of things to get sorted out in the flat, including more water, hot water, decent curtains, more furniture and kitchen equipment, and a new plug for the lamp.

Introduction to Omega Schools

Over the next few days I began to get a grip on things at Omega Schools, at least as far as my involvement was concerned. There was a meeting of the education team, which I sat in on but sadly failed to understand a lot of the issues being discussed. Since my expertise is in assessment and making test scores meaningful and useful, I began to look at some of the tests they were using in their schools, helped by Ato, a young man with some statistical expertise who was scheduled to work with me on this. I also looked at the results of a parental income survey he had run, searched on the Internet for socioeconomic data, and began to write a paper on a comparison between the socio-economic background of the Omega Schools families compared with Ghana as a whole.

I was given a PC to use in the office, but unfortunately I found it a real struggle to operate effectively, due to the frequent power cuts and also voltage fluctuations. Every time the voltage blipped even slightly, the PC would crash and I would have to wait while it rebooted. Then two minutes later, it went down again. Eventually the situation would be resolved by giving me a laptop with a battery backup which was charged by the mains (when available) but was not affected by voltage fluctuations. That made a great difference to my ability to write papers and set up data collection systems for test results.

I was beginning to get the hang of the Omega Schools setup. At that time they had 10 purpose-built schools in the area to the west of Accra, centred on the town of Kasoa which straddles the coast road a few miles west of Weija Junction. Ken was the CEO and Andrew the head of teaching and learning under him. He had a team of education specialists, each responsible for a different subject area. They oversaw the production of teaching materials and developed tests in their subjects, and also were responsible for inspecting the quality of teaching in the schools.

In contrast to the government school teachers, who were qualified, well-paid and had jobs for life, Omega teachers were unqualified high school graduates on low salaries, and with minimal job security. They were supplied with teaching materials and were expected to follow these closely – in other words, they had a precise 'script' for each lesson. These materials were initially developed by staff at one of the higher education institutions in Ghana, but as we were to discover, they were of very variable quality.

Parents paid by the day to send their children to one of these schools – one cedi a day (about 30p). Despite the fact that they had the option of sending their children to a government school for free, Omega Schools were extremely popular and there were long queues at the school entrance each morning as children handed in their cash for the day.

When I asked why this should be, I was told that government schools were extremely unpopular. Teachers tended to live a long way away and either turn up late or not at all. Because they had a guaranteed job they would often pay little attention to the children, and sometimes be asleep at their desk. Parents liked paying a small amount for their children's schooling, as it made them feel they had some control and would be listened to if there were problems. In addition, at an Omega school children got a free lunch each day, free uniform and books, all of which would have to be paid for at a government school. We were assured that when you take this into account, there was little difference in cost between the two types of school.

During my first week, Erica (science subject specialist) offered to take me with her as she visited a couple of the Omega schools. We got a taxi along the coast road to the market town of Kasoa, and then headed into the back streets. The taxi dropped us off and we made our way on foot through the narrow alleys until we reached the school. It was built to the standard Omega design: an enclosed courtyard surrounded by two storey buildings built roughly of concrete blocks. The classrooms had narrow windows without glass, and each accommodated about 50 pupils sitting at low desks, wearing their school uniforms — yellow t-shirts with the Omega symbol on the front, and dark shorts or skirts.

The classes in Omega schools include K1 and K2 (kindergarten - about 4 and 5 years old), P1 to P6 (primary — about 6 to 11) and JH1 to JH3 (junior high — about 12 to 14). We wandered from class to class, and in each one we entered the children stood up and greeted us in unison. The classes seemed crowded and very basic, but the pupils appeared hard-working and attentive. In some of the classes Erica spoke to the teacher about their teaching methods, quite often in subjects other than science.

From there we walked to the main road, guided by an older pupil, and got another taxi to school 94, in another area of Kasoa, which apparently has a large Muslim population. There seemed to be good relations between Christians and Muslims, and many Muslim parents send their children to Omega Schools, although they have a clear Christian ethos. We did a similar grand tour there, and then walked back through the market area to the main highway. We got a tro-tro (beat-up minibus) back to Weija Junction, and another (very rickety) taxi back to the office.

The long road to hot water

Back at the flat, just after arriving home on my first day I had an influx of people who had come to see about the hot water problem. These included colleagues from work plus the lady from next door who actually owned the flats. Her name was Elizabeth, and we got to know her quite well later. The consensus was that we needed to get a plumber in, so they promised to summon one to come tomorrow.

Next morning (Saturday) the plumber arrived. He came on foot with a small bag of tools, not in a van with his name on the side as we would expect in England. He clambered about on the water tanks on the roof, and then explained that the problem was lack of water pressure. The mains water in Ghana is erratic (like the electricity), so most houses have large black plastic back-up tanks on the roof to collect water when available and supply it to the house. However, the pressure from the tank was not enough to get the water up into the water heater, which was why there was no hot water. The solution was to install a pump to boost the water pressure.

He went off, and it was several days later that another plumber turned up with a pump and installed it. With it running, the kitchen tap worked brilliantly but the bathroom taps were still the same and there was no hot water. The plumber said we needed a bigger pump and went away again.

Time passed, and about a week later a third plumber turned up to inspect the system. He went off, and the next day plumber number 2 came back with a new pump and installed it. We waited till the power came on and then tested it. Amazing – good pressure from every tap and hot water! I had a luxurious hot shower to celebrate. Later he had to come back to fix a leak from the water heater, but other than that the system seemed to work well.

Ken had supplied me with a Ghanaian SIM card for my mobile phone, and also a dongle for the laptop so I could connect to the internet via another SIM card, and these appeared to work well. It seems to me that mobile phone technology has been a boon to developing countries, where the old infrastructure of phone lines and fixed communication links hardly exists. For a few cedis a month I was able to phone, check emails and Skype home to Sandie. She was finding it tough living in cramped conditions and waiting for the new baby to arrive. We were both feeling the strain of separation, especially as our wedding anniversary fell during the month.

I was using my laptop extensively, both to sort out the mass of photos from our South America trip at home and to do papers for work, but soon after I arrived the hard drive failed. I saw Eddy, the Omega Schools IT expert, who offered to replace the hard drive. Fortunately I had backed up our personal files on to a portable drive fairly recently, so only had about a week's worth of stuff to re-create. The moral is to back things up as often as possible! Eddy replaced the drive, but in the process installed a version of Windows 7 which kept sending me messages saying it was a bootleg copy and should be replaced! I ignored these messages, and nothing bad happened.

Out and about

My first expedition on my own was to walk to Shoprite, 4 or 5 miles away. To get there I had to walk through the narrow lanes to the main dirt road, go down the steep hill to the outskirts of Oblogo, and then turn left and along the road to the Coast Road at Weija Junction – this journey took about half an hour. I then walked along the main road to the supermarket, taking in all the sights and sounds of life in Ghana as I went along – the careering traffic, roadside stalls, brightly dressed women and people carrying enormous loads on their heads.

At Shoprite I loaded up my rucksack with basic supplies and headed back. I passed the aftermath of a fairly horrific road accident, and remembered

that the guidebook said the biggest danger in Ghana was not malaria or mugging, but road accidents, as they all drive like maniacs in clapped out vehicles. I began to see the truth in that. I also met up with a smartly dressed wedding party emerging from a church, and they chatted to me in a very friendly fashion as we crossed the road together.

Road accident aftermath

The following Saturday I went back to Shoprite, but this time I took a 'tro-tro' from Weija Junction. Tro-tros are a fascinating Ghanaian institution and we got to know them very well, and I will discuss them in more detail later. At the supermarket I went a bit mad, buying loads of supplies to keep me stocked up. Then at the checkout I discovered it came to more than I had money to pay for, so I had to leave a fair amount of stuff behind, which was rather embarrassing. I then only had enough cash to get a taxi to the foot of the hill, and had to struggle up the dirt road with my heavy bags of shopping. A schoolgirl took pity on me and helped me with the bags for part of the way – her good deed for the day, helping a poor old white man!

On the third Saturday of my stay in Ghana I resolved to venture further afield, and go into Accra. I had five aims: to get some bedding, reading books, and a Sudoku book, to have spare keys cut and enjoy a decent lunch in a restaurant. Over breakfast I studied the guidebook entry for Accra, and then I walked down to Weija Junction once more. I was hoping to get a tro-tro to the city, but they were all full up and not stopping. In the end I found a taxi whose driver offered to take me to Nkrumah Circle for a reasonable fee. This is a giant roundabout, surrounded by stalls of all kinds and crowded with people and traffic. I discovered that Accra has no real centre, but is a sprawling city where the places you might want to go to are widely separated. I wandered past all the various stalls selling all manner of stuff, and found one selling secondhand books where I got myself a paperback.

I had identified a key-cutting place nearby, so I wandered along the Central Ring Road to find it. Of course, when I got there, it was closed. I had a drink in a café opposite and then went in search of the Payless Book Store, again found on the internet. I picked up a taxi and directed him to drive to the address I had, but when we arrived there was no sign of the place at all. Totally frustrated, I told the taxi driver to take me to the Accra Mall and he dropped me there. This is a smart American-style shopping mall, quite a contrast to most of the other areas of Accra that I had seen.

However, the array of shops is quite disappointing, as they tend to be mainly upmarket clothes and furniture shops, not stocking the things I was looking for. The only bookshop had a very limited range and no Sudoku. There is a big South African store called Game which has a wide range of goods, and I bought some king-sized bedding there. Then I looked round the restaurants and had lunch in one which advertised African cuisine. I had vegetables in garlic and yam chips, with a couple of glasses of white wine, followed by disgustingly sweet cappuccino. Afterwards I went to the Shoprite there, which is quite large, and got some food supplies, before going out to find a taxi back to Oblogo.

I found one quite quickly, though he quoted 30 cedis, because he said the traffic was bad. He was not wrong, though he tried to avoid the worst holdups on the main road by going round the back streets. We still ended up stuck in queues for ages because of roadworks and general chaos. It took about 1½ hours, and then I had to walk up the hill, because the driver refused to go up there. I got back at 3.30 and collapsed in a heap. I reckoned I had achieved 2½ out of my 5 aims, which was not too bad for a novice white man in Ghana.

Going to church

The following day (Sunday) I had been invited by Ken to attend his church, so I got up early and waited for him to pick me up. Then there was a knock on the door, and it was Isaac, one of our colleagues, who had been sent to take me there. We set off on foot down the hill, and then were given a lift to the main road by one of Isaac's friends. From there we picked up a taxi, which took us to Shoprite, to my surprise. We walked round to the church, which was just behind the supermarket.

The service was in a large hall, but next door there was the skeleton of a vast structure, clearly in process of construction. The hall was crowded with smartly dressed people, the women in the gorgeous coloured dresses they wear to go to church. It was clear why Ken had invited me – his baby daughter was being baptised during the service. Ken was dressed in local costume, with colourful Kente cloth, and looked a most imposing figure.

The pastor gave an impassioned sermon, and although much of what he said was perfectly fine (be nice and kind and generous to others), he said it very loudly and at considerable length. He also made a strong appeal for funds and gifts in kind to complete the massive edifice which was being built out back. As it was also his birthday there was a celebration of that as well, and the whole thing finally ground to a halt after about two hours. I stayed to shake hands with a load of people and have some cake, and then Isaac and I got a taxi back.

Latter days alone

On the 23rd I finally got the long-awaited news – Claire had had her baby and our second grandson Oscar had joined the family! I was also able to give good news in return – our second pump was working and we now had hot water! No-one back home seemed to appreciate the crucial importance of this, however.

Flooding at Oblogo

The following day we had a really wild storm, which caused flooding in Accra and sounded pretty apocalyptic up on our hill. I lay in bed all night listening to the thunder and the rain pelting down on the tin roof, and watching the regular lightning flashes light up the room. Ghana apparently has a wet season in May and a 'mini Wet' in October, but that year I think they got swapped over. The next day the courtyard at Oblogo school was awash, and pupils and teachers had to creep round the edges to get to their classrooms.

Halfway through the month they began to bring me lunch at work. This was the standard fare which was given to the children and staff at the school, and tended to frequently consist of the Ghanaian staples of *banku* or *fufu*, which are nearly identical dishes made from cassava. Both are lumps of white dough-like substance, with the taste of wallpaper paste, but enlivened with some kind of stew or broth in which they swim. I tried hard to persuade them not to bring me any meat with it, and although I eat fish the tilapia that was sometimes included was very bony and hard to manage. However, I was very grateful for the thought and the fact that I was regarded as a full member of the team.

My favourite Ghanaian dish was *red red*, a kind of bean stew with plantains which gets its name from the red colour of the palm oil in which it is cooked. Back at home I was getting pretty good at cooking over our two gas rings, and trying to find sources of local ingredients rather than relying on trips to Shoprite for everything.

In preparation for Sandie's arrival I was trying to get the flat sorted out as far as possible. Omega Schools offered to provide me with a TV, provided I paid for the installation of a suitable network. I did so, and one day a lorry picked me up with the TV and the installation man and took us up the hill – except that we had to get out and walk because it was too steep for the lorry with us on board. The installer set up a dish, and we had a working TV with an eclectic mix of channels. I put the TV set on one of the arm chairs as we had no TV stand.

The other thing that was delivered was a wardrobe, so we now had somewhere to put our clothes. The place was beginning to look more like home, and I felt that quite a lot had been achieved in the month I was there on my own.

Obrunni!

Chapter 3: Finding Our Feet

Together again

On November 1st I waited anxiously to hear that Sandie was on her way. Claire texted me to say she had checked in at Heathrow, but because she was flying via Rome she was not due to land in Accra till late evening. I was expecting Ken to take me to the airport to pick her up, but then he phoned to say he could not come, but he was sending a driver (Asante – the man who brought our wardrobe) to pick me up.

Time passed, and then I decided to go out to meet him in case he was unable to find our place in the dark. I walked down to the dirt road that ran down the hill to Oblogo, and then slipped in a pothole and twisted my ankle. Asante turned up, and he drove me back down the hill and headed for Accra. The traffic was horrendous due to all the roadworks on the outskirts of the city, and I was starting to be afraid that Sandie would arrive without anyone to meet her.

We fought our way through the traffic chaos and reached the airport at 10.30, and Sandie emerged at 11 pm, having had a stop at Lagos. Surprisingly, the drive back was much quicker, and we were at the flat in not much more than half an hour. We took the cases inside and Sandie collapsed in bed, having had a pretty long day.

The next morning, when she got up, she complained about the bed being very hard. We discovered later that mattresses in Ghana are universally made of foam rubber and sprung mattresses are unheard of. We spent a quiet day together, getting the flat straightened out and downloading photos on to the laptop. After lunch we went for a brief walk round the neighbourhood to show her where the shops and local bar were – with a drink at the latter. We bought a new light bulb for the lounge.

In the evening we had drinks on the balcony and watched the sunset, and I filled Sandie in on Omega Schools and their testing programme. We went in to cook dinner and had an early night.

Getting to grips with Omega

The following day we went down together to the Omega office. However, the main excitement there was a two-day football competition between the ten schools in the Omega chain, held on the barren field next to the school. We went out for the opening ceremony, and then retired to my desk inside to talk through what was happening in terms of assessment.

Omega Schools football competition

 Testing was big at Omega, but not well-directed. In the middle of each term the P1 to P6 students were given tests in English, mathematics and science, and at the end of term there were examinations in all subjects, and results were presented to parents in individual reports. However, although mid-term test scores were recorded, there was little attempt to interpret them, or use them to inform future teaching and learning.

Our challenge was to change that, and make formative assessment a central feature of Omega Schools' drive to improve student learning. Formative assessment, sometimes called 'assessment for learning', tries to make testing students not just an end in itself but a springboard to better teaching and learning, by informing teachers (and ideally students) about every individual's strengths and weaknesses in each subject and making sure that this information feeds into future pedagogy.

To do this effectively needs three main elements: good and appropriate tests; informative, timely and meaningful feedback of results; and willingness of teachers and others to make use of the feedback in structuring future teaching. All three of these elements were going to be a challenge for us at Omega.

Mid-term tests for P1 to P6 pupils had recently been run, and I had begun setting up data collection spreadsheets to analyse the results. There were different tests for every year group, with about 30 to 50 questions ('items' in the jargon of testing) in each. The questions were all 'multiple choice' – that is, the student had to tick one of four boxes which gave the correct answer to each question. This kind of question is easy to mark, and can be done automatically, but is perhaps better at testing rote learning rather than a pupil's understanding of a subject.

I had already realised that there were problems with most, if not all, of the tests that had been run. They were developed by the subject specialists, who were not experts in test development. Writing good tests is a highly skilled task, and people who are good teachers and knowledgeable in their subject do not necessarily have that particular skill set. Sandie and I sat down together to review the tests in detail, making notes of items where there were problems. We were unable to use the computer as our extension cable had been commandeered for the football tournament.

We soon amassed a large collection of problem questions on just about every test. In some cases the question was ambiguous and there were two or more correct answers. In others none of the answers given was correct. Sometimes there were issues with how the test had been printed, with questions or even whole pages missing. We carried on reviewing the tests the next day (Friday), and at the end of the day were persuaded out on to the football field to present prizes to some of the winners.

The next week we got our extension lead back and were able to type up our review notes and present them to the subject specialists. We discovered that they were about to embark on a new round of testing, and therefore the first set of tests we had looked at were redundant. I abandoned entering data from them and focused on developing different kinds of feedback based on the test results.

Meanwhile Sandie, with her editing skills, had been asked to spend some time reviewing the teaching materials which were the 'scripts' for teachers to use for each lesson. She was also provided with her own PC, and we were moved into a separate office by ourselves, facing each other across a single desk. This brought a whole new dimension to 'togetherness'!

Every Friday the education team had a meeting, which we sat in on. Often the subjects discussed were unfamiliar to us, but over the weeks we began to understand some of the issues and concerns that the team faced. It took us a while, however, to get to know everyone in the office, and their roles. We had to confess to each other that one of our problems was telling the various young black men from one another. This sounds very racist, but we decided that it was a natural human tendency, to identify people first by their most outstanding characteristics – in this case, young and black. As we got to know people we could learn to distinguish other features – shape of face, nose length, hair style and so forth, and became more confident in identifying our different colleagues.

To show that this works both ways, when I was first introduced to Elizabeth, our neighbour and landlady, she thought I was James Tooley, whom she had met previously. Now James is a lot younger and shorter than I am, and had a full head of black hair, whereas my hair was white and pretty vestigial. But again the distinguishing features were 'white and old(ish)' in our cases. Admittedly our colleagues had no trouble identifying us, as we were the only white folks around, apart from visitors from abroad.

James actually turned up in the middle of November, and spent a few days at Omega. We had a meeting with him and Ken to thrash out some of the issues with the testing programme. We agreed to focus on the mid-term tests for developing feedback, and leave the end of term exams till later. We showed them the draft feedback I had developed, and the next day showed it to the education team and talked them through it.

The following day, in the afternoon, we went to a teachers' meeting at Kasoa 94 school. About 70 young teachers, both male and female, crammed into quite a small room, with the usual glassless slats for windows – it quickly got quite warm. First of all, Andrew Ofosu-Dankyi addressed them, and did an exercise in groups to convince them of the necessity of doing the tests correctly, with no cheating. This was apparently a bit of a problem, with teachers convinced they were being judged on their pupils' test results, and helping them to give the correct answers.

After Andrew had finished it was our turn. We presented various examples of feedback and asked them to say which they would find most useful in their classroom teaching. It was hard to get much response from most of them, but a few of the more articulate ones showed a preference

Discussing the feedback

for one type of feedback or another. At the end of this session we came to the conclusion that we should produce as many different styles as possible, in the expectation that different teachers would prefer different ways of receiving their results.

After the meeting James took us back to his hotel, together with a woman called Caitlin from Pearson, who were helping to sponsor the work of Omega Schools. We sat outside and chewed the fat, and had some food. Later we got a taxi back to Top Base.

After the second round of mid-term testing, we needed to enter the test data in order to produce the feedback for teachers and school managers. This turned out to be a bit of a nightmare. Ato had arranged for the data to be collected from the schools, but it came in quite slowly. He had also arranged for a team of students to enter the data into the spreadsheets I had set up, and I had a session with them explaining how to do this. Despite this, the process went very slowly and with many errors. In the end Sandie and I got hold of large batches of data sheets and entered the data ourselves.

One of the big problems was identifying students and linking their results in English, maths and science. We had asked each teacher to give every student a unique identifying number and write this on each script, as well as their name. Unfortunately, this system failed in many cases – either numbers were missing or were inconsistent between subjects. I had to spend a lot of time matching pupils' results by name, which was also a frustrating task. In Ghana many people have at least three names, and often the pupils would write a different two on each script, possibly in a different order and with variable spelling. Is 'Gifty Bright' the same girl as 'Gifty Ofusu' or 'Ofosu Bright'?

Once we had as much data as we were likely to get (with missing schools, year groups and subjects) I put it all into my magic spreadsheets to produce feedback for each school and year group. There were two sets of feedback – one for teachers, showing how the pupils in their class were performing in each subject in some detail, and one for school managers showing how their school's results compared with Omega overall. Excruciatingly complete descriptions of the final feedback are given in Appendix A.

The remaining task was to print all this information, collate it and copy it to provide booklets for each teacher and school manager, as well as versions for the subject specialists. This was complicated by the quirky Omega printer, the temperamental network connection to it, and the fact that the printer was being used to produce vast amounts of teaching materials at the same time. We collated the booklets and sent them out to be copied and stapled, and they came back with the pages completely jumbled, so that had to be done again.

Eventually, working flat out, we got feedback for the school managers for every school bar one. That afternoon we got a taxi to Kasoa 94 school for a meeting with the managers, where we handed out their feedback and Sandie talked them through it. Afterwards Erica guided us through the screaming chaos which is Kasoa market, and we got a taxi home.

By now it was pretty well the end of term, and it was decided that giving feedback to teachers would have to wait till next term. We went to an end of term staff meeting, at which Ken harangued the troops about getting workbooks ready for next term. After that we began to look forward to flying home for Christmas, having achieved some progress but not as much as we might have hoped.

One day in December Sandie and I were invited to a carol concert at another school. I had to stay at home, waiting for a plumber. I kept getting texts from her, saying it was going on for ever, and updated her about progress at home. Apparently the concert started late, and every one of the ten schools had to perform for a considerable time. She finally made it back home just in time for sunset drinks.

Omega Schools carol concert

Challenges and triumphs at the flat

Although I had managed to get some things organised in the flat, there was still a lot to be done. For example, in the bedroom the curtains for two of the windows were just draped across the windows' security grills and could not be easily drawn. The third window had no curtain, but I had draped a bedspread over it using a rope as a curtain rail – none of this was either elegant or practical.

We met Elizabeth, our nextdoor neighbour and owner of the block of flats. She was in her 70s and had lived in the USA for a while, and had an extensive family in and around Accra. She also ran a nursery school on her premises, and from our balcony we could look down into the courtyard and watch the children turning up in the morning, and in the evening doing their closing ceremony, standing in serried ranks and chanting their final prayer.

Elizabeth came to see us and said that the tenants of the flat below ours were complaining of water pouring down the wall from our flat. It transpired that our new pump had boosted the pressure in our system to such an extent that it had sprung a leak and was now causing problems for those downstairs. Elizabeth's grandson eventually organised plumbers to come and fix it, and they turned up a couple of days later. They had to dig some pipework out of the shower and replace it, which repaired the leak but left a bit of a hole in the wall of the shower. They were supposed to come back to re-tile it, but it was quite a while before that happened. Meanwhile we could again have hot water without flooding the neighbours.

The first weekend after Sandie arrived we had a 48-hour power cut, which was a bit of a trial. Fortunately we were out quite a lot of the time, but the fridge completely defrosted. There was not a lot in there that spoiled (an advantage of being vegetarian). Obviously we had no hot water for that period. The 'normal' power cuts tended to be 4 hours long, and were clearly due to load shedding because of insufficient capacity in the power system (despite the massive Volta hydroelectric dam which we saw later on). However, we guessed that longer power cuts were due to major equipment failures, though fortunately they were much less frequent than the shorter blackouts.

Our next challenge was getting our washing done. I had done some of my own by hand in the sink, but we did not feel this was a sustainable plan for the long term. We made enquiries at work and were told we should get ourselves a cleaner, who would clean the flat and do our washing for us. Erica promised to find one for us, and the next Saturday a young woman called Betsy turned up with two small children in tow. She explained she was our new cleaner, though her English was not good, and we moved out on to the balcony and left her to it. She cleaned the flat and did our washing by hand, and after 2½ hours came out to say she had finished.

We asked her how much she wanted, and after a bit of a struggle understood her to say 150 cedis. It was difficult to make out what she wanted exactly, as the cedi had just been revalued, and this seemed a bit steep. But being naïve and not knowing any better we gave her that much and off she went. We checked with Erica, who said we had been massively ripped off, probably because of being dumb white foreigners. She went to see Betsy and harangued her about it, but she could not repay any of the money because it had already been spent. Erica got her to agree to come every Saturday to clean for us in order to pay off the debt, and that is what happened.

Every Saturday morning Betsy would arrive with her two kids, and we would sit out on the balcony while she cleaned the flat and did our washing. We did not want to go out and leave her there alone, as after the incident with the money we did not entirely trust her. However, it meant we were tied there every Saturday, which was rather a pain. After several weeks like this we agreed we needed a different solution to the problem of getting our clothes washed. I was quite happy to do the weekly cleaning, so we just needed some easier way of doing the washing.

Meanwhile, another challenge involved water for drinking and cooking. We had been warned that the mains water was too heavy in minerals to drink safely, especially for non-locals. Ken had supplied us with several 2-litre bottles of mineral water, but when these got used up we realised they would have been quite expensive to buy at Shoprite. The solution was to buy what the locals did – purified water in 500cc pouches. These came in large bags containing 30 pouches, which therefore weighed 15 kilograms. Our strategy was to go to the nearest local shop which supplied these pouches and buy a bag, and then split the pouches between our two rucksacks and carry them back to the flat. Then I would decant the pouches into the empty 2-litre bottles and we would use that water for drinking and cooking.

We also traced sources of supply for other kinds of drink. Wine could be bought from Shoprite, and from some of the little shops in Oblogo. There was also a shop which sold local (Kasapreko) gin as well as bottles of tonic. He would only sell a minimum of half a case (12 bottles), so again we would load up the rucksacks and carry them up the hill to home. At another shop we could get bottles of local Star beer, which Sandie liked, so we were able to stock up for our regular evening sundowners.

On our return from the office, hot and sweaty having climbed the hill, we would jump in the shower (if the power was on) and then watch the regular 6 o'clock sunset from our balcony. We had moved a small plastic table and two plastic chairs out there, and that was where we had breakfast as well as sundowners. I had a gin and tonic, while Sandie had half a large bottle of Star beer – we would decant the other half into an empty tonic bottle for the next night.

As Ghana is only just north of the equator, sunset was virtually constant at 6 pm, all through the year. We would sit there and chill, and watch the kids next door going home from their day at nursery. Often we would see flights of egrets overhead, heading for their night-time roosting sites near the coast. Flocks of vultures circled over the nearby hills.

Sunset drinks

Our balcony faced north-west, and beyond the hill on which we were perched were other lines of hills, each covered with a variety of dwellings from smart mansions to mere shacks. As the sun went down we would see the lights go on over there, and then quite

In the lounge

often (usually just after 6) they would suddenly all go off again, and we would know they were having a power cut. Frequently ours would go off soon after, and we would be left in the dark until about 10 pm.

In the middle of November our patron James Tooley arrived in Ghana to visit Omega Schools. He and Ken came round in the evening and sat on our balcony to join in the sunset drinks, and we talked between ourselves for quite a while. During that session they agreed to give Sandie an allowance, to take account of the work she was doing for Omega, and also to pay us 1000 cedis to buy furniture and equipment for the flat. We were delighted and grateful, because now we could turn the place from an indoor campsite into a home.

On our next trip to Accra we visited the massive Game store and priced up various options. With our 1000 cedi budget we finally decided to buy a washing machine as our first priority, which would free us from the need to employ someone like Betsy and enable us to wash our clothes as and when we wanted. We also decided to get a coffee table and TV stand, as well as more bedding, bath mats, a toaster and curtain rails for the bedroom. We went back to Game and ordered all these things, and that was the 1000 cedis gone!

The next challenge was to get all these items to our flat. Sadly, we were outside the delivery zone for Game, but Ken agreed to send a lorry to pick the stuff up for us. We said they would need two men to carry the washing machine up the stairs, but when Sandie went round to wait for the arrival of the lorry, she found there was just a driver. Not to worry – he picked up the washing machine, put it on his head, and carried it up to the flat like that. We soon realised that this was the way things were usually carried in Ghana. When I got home I assembled the coffee table and TV stand, and now the TV set could be moved off its armchair to reside proudly on its very own stand!

The final hurdle to be overcome was getting someone to plumb in the washing machine and put up the curtain rails. By now I was getting used to the experience of contacting somebody, arranging for them to come, them not showing up, arranging another day, and so forth. After several days of this a plumber/handyman did turn up, while I was there, and succeeded in plumbing in the washing machine. I then asked him to use his drill to put up the curtain rails, which was quite a tough job as the walls were very hard. In the end between us we installed all three curtain rails in the bedroom. I paid the man and he went off, and I danced for joy before returning to work.

Later on we put curtain hooks in the two curtains we already had and another we had bought from a local shop, and fitted them to the rails. The bedspread held up with rope came down, and now we could open and shut the bedroom curtains at will.

Now, about six weeks since Sandie arrived, we had turned the flat into quite a pleasant home. There would continue to be things to fix and add to make it more comfortable, but we were fairly content with what had been achieved.

Chapter 4: Out and About

Kokrobite Beach

After Sandie arrived, we spent our weekends exploring further afield. The first Sunday we resolved to go to the nearby beach, at Kokrobite. To get there was a bit of a mission, but over time we became adept at finding

our way. First we had to walk down the hill to the main road at Weija Junction, passing a number of smartly-dressed women on their way to church. From there we took a tro-tro to another junction a couple of miles along called 'Old Barrier'. On the corner there a number of battered taxis were waiting, going to different destinations, which would head off once they were full with four passengers. We would find one going to Kokrobite and wait for a couple of other passengers.

Going to church

The road was paved to start with, but soon it became pretty rough and we jolted along over the potholes in intimate contact with the person next to us. Eventually we reached the centre of Kokrobite village and disembarked. The first time there we had to ask the way to the beach, and were pointed down a dirt track which eventually brought us to the sea.

When we reached the beach, it was covered in white bodies. The bodies belonged to young volunteers who were working in schools and hospitals around Accra, and who came to the beach on Sunday, just like us.

The beach was in fact a multi-use area, with white bikini-clad youngsters, fishing boats pulled up, local boys playing football or swimming in the sea, and traders selling their wares to the sunbathers. Often there were many local women with racks of secondhand clothes set out on the sand, and young white females busily trying them on. There were also stalls selling local crafts, and one man with a stall full of handbags, where Sandie became a regular customer later.

Kokrobite Beach

Once we had become acclimatised to the spectacle we found a spare patch of sand away from the football games and sunbathed for a bit. I went in the sea, which was warm but full of rubbish, in particular black plastic bags. Every time you buy something in Ghana they insist on putting it into a black plastic bag, and these blow around everywhere. A large number manage to find their way into the sea, where they float around like black jellyfish.

After a while we went for a walk east along the beach, past all the brightly painted fishing boats drawn up on the sand. Further along we were stopped by a security guard, who warned us not to go any further, as the people to the east would rob us. We were dubious, as we had heard that Ghana was a pretty safe place, but turned back. Maybe he was being over-cautious, or wanted us to stay and spend our money on his bit of beach.

Next to the beach is an establishment known as Big Milly's Backyard, a kind of low-grade beach resort with a café, a bar, an upstairs viewing area, more stalls and some basic accommodation. We went in, got drinks and a packet of biscuits from the bar for lunch, and sat there for a bit, before returning to the beach. Later we went back to Big Milly's and got cocktails from a little bar underneath the viewing deck, and then sat up there watching life on the beach.

Obrunni!

When it was time to go we got a tro-tro all the way back to Weija Junction and walked home up the hill. To our amazement the 48-hour power cut we had been experiencing was finally over!

Weija

The next day was a national holiday for Independence Day, and in the afternoon we decided to explore the road through Oblogo in the direction of Weija. We went down the hill and began walking to the right, away from the Coast Road. We had the usual cries of 'Obrunni!' on the way from the people we passed, and after about half an hour we reached a fairly smart bar by the road called Daddy's Cottage. We stopped for a drink there and then pressed on.

Weija itself was similar to Oblogo – a scattering of shacks, with some better-looking houses, spread along the road and into the countryside on either side. We were looking for Weija Lake, and at a junction we asked a woman for directions and she said "Follow me". She took us down a narrow footpath and then began scrambling over boulders at the foot of the dam. I stopped and waited, because it was hurting my leg, but Sandie went on with her as far as the river by the dam, where she took some photos and then came back to join me. We returned to Weija, and had another drink in Daddy's Cottage before walking back to the flat.

Exploring Accra

During the two months before Christmas we made several trips into Accra. The city tends to sprawl, without a clearly defined centre, and it was necessary to make separate excursions to different districts within the urban area.

On our first joint visit to Accra, we got a taxi to the Jamestown area, near the sea. We walked along the seafront to the lighthouse, and then went down to the Jaynii beach bar, which supports local children going to school. It was pretty quiet when we were there, but we had a drink and chatted to the proprietress and her husband before moving on.

Mantse Palace

We tried to visit the Mantse Palace over the road, but got chased away by a guard and told not to take photos of the outside. We walked down to the fishing harbour below the fort, which was pretty scruffy, but instantly got hassled by someone wanting to guide us. So we turned round and quit, and then carried on walking up the main road towards the centre of the city. We passed Usher Town (also scruffy) and then got into more modern and smarter areas. We passed the Cathedral, and then walked along the main road towards the National Theatre.

The National Theatre building is very smart, but it was impossible to find out what performances were happening there. Finally we found someone who gave us his phone number, and said that by Monday or Tuesday they might have a programme for the week! Later we tried ringing but got nowhere, and the website for the theatre gave no information. An ongoing problem during our stay in Ghana was finding information about programmes of events, including TV schedules.

From the National Theatre we got a taxi to the Accra Mall – we could stop coming back there for a touch of civilisation any time we liked! We went to Tante Marie's African restaurant for lunch, and although the food was not too exciting it was good to sit down somewhere fairly smart and be waited on. After shopping in Game and Shoprite, we got a taxi back to Top Base.

The following Sunday we took a taxi to La Beach, on the far side of the city. We had to pay to go on the beach, which was totally covered in beach bar after beach bar, with serried ranks of chairs and loungers. There was hardly any sand to be seen. We had a drink at one bar and wandered

about a bit, and then established a base camp at another bar with occasional forays into the sea. We had lunch there, and I ordered 'lobster and chips', which turned out to be a kind of crayfish, but very tasty. After a while there we got a

Lobster and chips

taxi to the Accra Mall as usual, and then home after shopping.

Our next venture into the capital took us to the area of Osu and the Cantonments Road, locally known as 'Oxford Street'. It is meant to be the most happening part of town, with many bars and restaurants, but it was fairly quiet on a Sunday. We visited the Koala supermarket, which has imported goods at very high prices, and found a 'British' pub, where I got a pretty reasonable lunch of fish and chips. Afterwards it was our usual pilgrimage to Accra Mall.

Tro-tros

In Ghana most public transport is by privately-owned minibuses, or 'tro-tros'. The name apparently comes from the local Ga word 'tro', meaning 'three', as in colonial days the fare was three pence per journey. At first we were unsure about them, as they seemed rather rickety, and by reputation were frequently involved in accidents due to the maniacal way they were driven

However, if we wanted to explore the country or even the local neighbourhood, it became obvious that we had to get used to them. Taxis were useful, especially when carrying lots of shopping, but became expensive for longer journeys. So we soon got acclimatised to using the tro-tros, and swiftly became quite experienced.

Tro-tros are secondhand minibuses, many bought from Germany (judging by the logos on the side) with three or four rows of seats. They have a driver and a mate, who leans out of the sliding door at the side and shouts the destination, and also makes hand signals. There are regular stopping places along the road, but if the mate sees anyone he thinks might want to get on he will tell the driver to stop.

In a tro-tro

Inside, tro-tros are often in pretty bad shape, with loose fabric hanging from the ceiling and battered seats. Frequently they are plastered with religious posters and have slogans like 'Trust the Word of Jesus' emblazoned across the front or rear windows. There is a narrow gangway leading to the rear rows of seats, but when the vehicle if full this is blocked by passengers sitting on folding seats. The mate will try to encourage people to sit at the back to leave space in the front row. If people at the back want to get off, then quite often half the bus has to disembark to let them leave.

Fares are very reasonable – one or two cedis (30p or 60p). Paying your fare can be quite a process, if the tro-tro is full. The mate stays at the front and passengers at the back pass their money forward to him, and get their change passed back. Those in the middle rows can have a fulltime job passing notes and coins to and fro.

Tro-tros are driven with total disregard for anyone else on the road, cutting up other traffic with wild abandon and frequently racing each other to the next stop. We saw several tro-tro wrecks by the roadside during our year in Ghana. They can also be in a poor state of repair – on one occasion the side door almost fell off our vehicle as it was negotiating a roundabout, and the mate had to hang on to it for the rest of the journey.

Catching a tro-tro can be exciting at busy times. A large crowd will gather at the stop, and when one appears with the mate shouting the desired destination, everyone surges forward at once. Queuing is unknown, and we had to learn to abandon our western politeness and be prepared to use our elbows to get anywhere.

The tro-tros I have described so far were the local 'stopping' tro-tros. In addition there were long distance tro-tros, as we discovered later. These start from a fixed point, where there is a man at a desk selling tickets for the desired destination, and you climb on board the vehicle and wait until it is full, when it sets off. It will drop people off before the final destination, but does no pick-ups until after there are empty seats on board.

These tro-tros were to become our preferred mode of long-distance transport when exploring further afield from Accra.

Cape Coast and Elmina

Our only distant excursion before Christmas was a long weekend on the coast to the west of Accra, visiting the towns of Cape Coast and Elmina. Friday 2nd December was a public holiday (Farmers' Day) so we took a tro-tro to Kaneshie Market in Accra, and then a taxi to the STC bus station to catch a scheduled bus to Cape Coast. Although the buses passed through Weija Junction on the way west, they did not stop to pick up passengers, unless they already had tickets, so this was the only option we thought we had.

We arrived at the bus station at 10 am and were told there was a bus at 12.30, so we got drinks and settled down to wait. 12.30 came and went, with no sign of a bus. Eventually one appeared at 12.45, and we discovered this was the one to Takoradi, which had been combined with the Cape Coast one. We got on, and it finally left at 1.15. The traffic going back was diabolical, and it took us two hours to get back to Weija Junction, where we had started 6 hours before! The bus then speeded up, and got to the bus station outside Cape Coast just after 5 pm.

A taxi took us into the town and up to Prospect Lodge, where we had booked a room. This is perched on a hill overlooking the town, with spectacular views from its terrace. However, they claimed to have only big bottles of beer to drink there, so set off down the hill to explore the town. Tropical night fell, and we reached an area with no lighting and decided not to continue. Going back, we reached a junction with a large statue of a crab (the city's mascot) in the centre and a noisy local bar nearby. We got drinks and sat outside by the street and watched the colourful local life go by.

From there we got a taxi to the 'Mighty Victory' Hotel, and went in for dinner. The dining room was soulless and quite empty, but we had a reasonable meal. Sandie is a vegetarian, but I eat fish and seafood as well, She managed to get a vegetarian dish and I had lobster and chips, which became one of my favourite meals in Ghana. Another taxi took us back to our hotel and we sat on the terrace for a bit, as our room was fairly dark, before going to bed.

On Saturday breakfast on the Prospect Lodge terrace was reasonable, if slow – omelette and toast, with tea/coffee. We went out, walking down the main road towards the sea and the white bulk of Cape Coast Castle. We found the Blackstar Bookshop near the castle and went in, and bought three Dick Francis novels to supplement our reading materials.

Leaving Cape Coast Castle till the morrow, we took a taxi along the coast to Elmina, and were dropped off near the castle there, where we picked up a guided tour. Elmina was a slave castle built by the Dutch and run by them for most of its history, though taken over by the British later. The guide was good, and showed us the slave dungeons and explained the horrific history of the place. The way the slaves were treated there before being packed into ships like sardines and sent to the Americas was truly disgusting. I began to feel ashamed of my Dutch ancestry.

From the castle there were panoramic views over the town and the fishing boats drawn up under the walls. Afterwards we had drinks at a nearby cafe, and then walked up to Fort Jago on a nearby hill. We tipped the men who were apparently guarding the place, and were able to get in and have

Elmina

a look round, with more extensive views over the town from the walls.

Posuban shrine

After our visit to the fort we passed four of the 'posubans', which are a combination of shrine and storehouse for local militia groups, and decorated with some rather weird statues. One posuban had a full-scale ship model on top, and another had statues of Adam and Eve. On our walk round we encountered a couple of funeral celebrations and a wedding, with rows of plastic chairs arranged in the open for guests to use. Later on we would often see these 'plastic chair events', as we came to call them.

Having exhausted the delights of Elmina, another taxi brought us back to Cape Coast, and we were dropped off near the castle there. The nearby Baobab cafe, which is a kind of charitable foundation run by Germans, has an extensive veggie menu. We had a pleasant lunch there, and also looked in the craft shop, where Sandie bought a dress and a mug as a gift. Afterwards we went back to the hotel and showered, and chilled for a bit.

On the beach

We went out again and walked down to the coast. On the way, Sandie got her foot run over by a car in the busy main street (there are no pavements to speak of), but was still able to carry on walking. We went down to the Oasis Beach Resort, and sat at a table overlooking the beach, watching the people splashing in the surf and the sun setting. We had a couple of drinks and pizzas there. An acrobatic/break dance troupe started up, making an extremely loud noise. We walked back to the hotel, and watched a film on TV.

After breakfast on the terrace the next day, we packed up and checked out, and walked down to the Cape Coast Castle to do the tour there. This was similar to Elmina, with more dungeons etc., though British rather than Dutch. The 'Door of No Return' was where slaves went out to get into the ships that would take them over the ocean, and nearby was a plaque commemorating a recent visit by Barack and Michelle Obama – she believes that her ancestors passed through that door.

Cape Coast and the castle

This time, I was shamed by my British ancestry, though it was pointed out that the local inhabitants were the ones who captured and sold the slaves, so the guilt has to be shared to some extent.

When we emerged we looked round the craft stalls in the courtyard, and then went next door to the Castle restaurant, with a table overlooking the beach and the waves crashing on the rocks. We had drinks first, and then ordered food. I had lobster thermidor and chips, which was nice, and Sandie had roast veggies and chips, which she enjoyed. After lunch we went back to the hotel to collect our rucksack, and then went round to the Metro Mass station and bought tickets. Since Cape Coast is the western terminus for this bus line, it is possible to board a bus here to be dropped off along the way to Accra.

There was a bus there for Accra, so we got on at about 1 pm. We then had a long wait while it filled up with passengers, and it finally left at 1.50. The journey to Weija Junction took just over two hours.

Socialising

Although Ghanaians are very friendly, we did not get many invitations to socialise with them in their homes. An exception was Erica, the science specialist at Omega, who became a good friend and invited us to have lunch with her at her home. She arranged for a taxi to pick us up from Weija Junction and take us to her house in Kasoa one Saturday in November. The traffic on the Coast Road in Kasoa was dreadful, as usual, and we got stuck there for a while.

When we arrived she showed us round her pleasant home and gave us lunch, with a wide variety of dishes catering to our dietary preferences. This was a great opportunity to stay and chat to a well-educated Ghanaian, and we thoroughly enjoyed it. Afterwards the taxi took us back to Weija Junction and we walked home.

We had visited our neighbour and landlady Elizabeth a couple of times and got to know her quite well. She told us she had spent some times in the USA and then returned to Ghana, and had quite an extensive family living in the Accra area, including two sons who were both ministers of religion. She invited us to attend her birthday party, on a Saturday afternoon in December.

It was due to start at 1 o'clock, and they had put up awnings and chairs next door, but there was no sign of other guests, so we waited till about 3 o'clock before going round. Elizabeth and her family greeted us warmly

– the other guests were apparently stuck in traffic. We had soft drinks and nibblies, and then a sound system appeared (with a generator as the power was off) and there was music and some dancing. More guests gradually appeared, and then we had some food. Afterwards Elizabeth was presented with a car by her children, and cut her birthday cake. As there were no lights, when it got dark we went and sat outside, in the light of a car's headlamps. We left about 8

Elizabeth and family

o'clock, and then sat on our balcony with drinks, listening to the party going on next door.

The next day (Sunday) we were invited to attend a thanksgiving service for her at her son's church to the north of Accra. We were due to leave at 7 am, but after we turned up there was a lot of hanging about and we didn't leave till about 7.45, squeezed into a car with Elizabeth, the driver, a daughter and two small grandsons. We drove into Accra, round the bypass, and then north up to Madina. We got there just before 9 o'clock, and sat about in his house for about an hour while they did assorted preparations.

About 10 o'clock we processed round to the church, where the service was in full swing. It was interesting and typical of Ghanaian evangelical Christianity, as we came to recognise it – very charismatic, with people jumping about and babbling, and very noisy. The theology was fundamentalist, but Elizabeth was celebrated and got to cut her cake again. Afterwards we sat in the son's office for a bit before driving back. The traffic was quite heavy, but we returned home just before 3 pm, to find the power off again. In all these celebrations we were the only white people present, but were treated with great friendliness and as honoured guests.

Before heading back to England for Christmas we decided to host a little drinks party in our flat for friends and colleagues. In the end almost all the staff from the Omega office turned up, and sat around chatting and drinking soft drinks for about an hour. A large number of Ghanaians are teetotal, so we had to make sure there was plenty of non-alcoholic refreshment to give them. Before they left, we had to have a prayer together – altogether a different experience from a similar event in Britain!

Heading home for Christmas

My first three months were up, and we had reached an agreement with James that we would return after Christmas, with him paying for our flights in future, as well as our insurance.

Obrunni!

On 23rd December, at 2.30, a taxi came for us, and took us into the city by back roads, avoiding the jams at the roadworks. Unfortunately, we got a bit stuck when we got near the airport, and after one and a half hours the driver dropped us at the Shangri-La Hotel, later renamed Western Sun. We left our luggage and went to the pool for a couple of hours, which was OK (though the gents' changing room was not very pleasant). Afterwards we sat on the hotel verandah for about three hours, having drinks and a meal (quite nice pizzas), followed by coffee and cocktails. A group was playing quite pleasant variations on Christmas music in the grounds, but we were pretty much the only customers.

At 9 pm we got a shuttle from the hotel to the airport, and checked in for the flight to Rome. We had to go through immigration, where they suddenly dragged me out of the queue and took me to an office, where they announced we were only allowed to stay for 60 days at a time, despite having one-year visas – something we had never been informed about. Sandie was all right, because she had been in the country less than 60 days, but she insisted on accompanying me into the office. I had to pay a fine, and then we ran the gauntlet of security before finally escaping into the departure lounge.

The flight boarded and left on time at 11.45, but we had a few problems with the plane. Sandie's seat was broken and quite uncomfortable, and the toilets were in bad shape. They gave us dinner some time after take-off, but no breakfast. We landed in Rome at 6.10, and eventually found our way through security to the main concourse, where we had coffee and croissants for breakfast. The flight to London left on time and landed us back in Heathrow at about 11 am on Christmas Eve. After immigration and baggage claim, we went out to where our daughter Claire was waiting with our two young grandsons.

Our accommodation over Christmas was a small hotel, Abbey Lodge, which we had stayed in before and found very comfortable. The house where Claire lived with her sons and partner was too small for us to squeeze into as well, so apart from the flat in Ghana we were NFA (no fixed abode). Our younger son Paul had travelled down from Manchester for Christmas, so he was staying in the same hotel.

45

Obrunni!

On Christmas Day the three of us went round to Claire's house and had a relaxing day together, eating, drinking, watching films and overseeing Charlie (aged 2½) opening his shedloads of presents. On Boxing Day our elder son Andrew drove over with his wife and two daughters to join us, and the family was shuttled over to Marlow-on-Thames where we had booked a table for the whole 11 of us to have a family meal together.

On 29th December we went to Luton Airport to catch a flight up to Glasgow, to see my Aunt Margie who had had a stroke. We visited her in Gartnavel Hospital, and found she was able to talk well though unhappy about being incapacitated. That evening we stayed in the Pond Hotel next to the hospital. The following morning we took the train into Glasgow city centre and did a bit of shopping, before returning to the hospital in time for afternoon visiting. Then it was a taxi to the airport and an evening flight back to Luton.

The rest of our time in England was mainly taken up with shopping for stuff to take back to Ghana, visiting friends, and catching up with TV programmes that we had missed. On 4th January it was time to go to Heathrow to catch the flight back to Ghana.

Chapter 5: Back in Harness

Home Sweet Home

After Christmas, James had agreed to book our flights for us, so we for our return in January 2012 we could fly British Airways direct to Accra. The flight takes about six hours, straight over the top of the Sahara desert, and we landed at 8.45 pm. We had rung Alex, the taxi driver who had brought us to the airport before Christmas, and he picked us up once we had emerged from Immigration and collected our bags.

We had discovered that Alex lived quite near us on Gbawe Top Base, so in the months to come he drove us around quite a lot, picking us up when we had a load of shopping or taking us places when we had luggage, or did not want to walk back up the hill in the dark. Most other taxi drivers complained bitterly about driving us up the rough dirt road to home, but Alex and his battered cab were obviously inured to it.

One of the items we had packed in the three cases we had brought this time was the airbed we used when camping, plus a pump. The next day we blew it up and placed it on top of the hard Ghanaian mattress, to give ourselves a softer sleeping platform. It looked rather strange lying there, as it was smaller than the enormous king-sized bed underneath, and it

 was a bit of a climb to get on top. I remarked that it reminded me of the step-pyramid of King Zoser, which we had seen in Egypt many years before. If either of us landed on the mattress too hard, we were likely to bounce the other one off on to the floor – but we did

Our pyramid bed   sleep better on top of our pyramid.

Each morning we woke up at 6 o'clock. This was not deliberate policy, but purely due to our surroundings. The sun came up then, and with the sun came the chickens, all crowing loudly to outdo each other. At the same time our neighbours turned on their radio to full volume; sleep was no longer an option. Of course, we slept with all the windows open so there was no way of cutting down the sound from outside.

Obrunni!

The day after our return we invited Elizabeth from next door and her family for drinks. About seven of them came over, and we had a pleasant time together, though they did not stay long and left about 7 o'clock. The next day a workman came round to replace the tiles in the bathroom that were wrecked when the plumbers fixed the leak before Christmas.

The next challenge was to set up a local bank account for ourselves, so Omega could pay our allowance into it, instead of handing over cash every week. We left work early and got a tro-tro to Old Barrier (the junction for Kokrobite), and went into the Ecobank branch there. Sandie spent a fair while setting up a bank account, and then even longer queuing to pay in cash to initiate it.

Three weeks later we got a message to say her bank card was ready, so we travelled back to the branch to pick it up. Needless to say, the staff had to hunt for the card, but eventually found it. However, there was no sign of the PIN we needed to get money out of the account. After more hassle we managed to get some cash out, but it was another week before the PIN arrived and we had to go down again to collect it. We began to realise this kind of experience was NFG (Normal For Ghana) and it was important not to let it stress us out. However, later on we were to have a long and bitter run-in with Ecobank, but that story comes in another chapter.

We were determined not to spend every evening at home, and to find places to go out for a meal or a drink. One Saturday night we went out and walked down to Weija Junction to try out a restaurant we had seen near there. However, they had nothing vegetarian so we got a shared taxi west along the coast road to the Chanel London Pub. This is an outdoor bar by the main road, with drinks and food. However, there was a very loud football match being broadcast and again nothing vegetarian to eat. We crossed the road to the Sizzler restaurant opposite, and found this was a relatively smart place on the first floor with proper tables and waiter service.

We had a bottle of nice South African wine and a pleasant meal – I discovered they served lobster thermidor and chips, which became my

48

standard there. Alex took us home, and after that the Sizzler became our regular venue for a local night out.

The next day (Sunday) we explored a new path down the hill which brought us out at Oblogo school and our office. As this was the most direct route we had found, it then became our standard way to get to and from

the office. It was fairly steep, and ended up taking us through a recycling yard, where (during the week) a number of people were working hard at great piles of scrap, sorting it and breaking it up to go into containers which were hauled away to be melted down. Each weekday as we went through we had a cheery greeting from these folk.

Down the hill to Oblogo

The same Sunday we decided to walk to Weija and explore Weija Lake, which we had heard about but never seen. However, when we got to the village we failed to find any way through to the lake, so we walked back to the coast road. We got a tro-tro to where the lake comes down to the road, and walked along the shoreline for a bit, finding another group of people furiously quarrying stone. We went on to Shoprite and did a bit of shopping before heading home.

The next excitement on the home front occurred halfway through February, when I noticed water dripping down from the big black storage tank on the roof. I spoke to Elizabeth about it, and she said it might be because the tank was full. We ran a load of water but the drip persisted. The next day a plumber turned up to inspect the tank. He climbed up to it and announced that it was going to be a big job to fix – the sheet the tank was standing on was rotten and would need to be replaced, or else the whole tank would fall down. I told him to contact Elizabeth.

A few days later we heard from Elizabeth that the tank would need to be replaced, and all the water first had to be drained out of it. We assumed this would be happening immediately, and filled up the bath to give us a backup water supply once the tank was empty and no more was flowing. In the meanwhile we kept taking water from the system, expecting that it would run out at any time, but it carried on flowing until the end of the month when we returned to the UK.

One evening later in February we discovered there was some kind of religious extravaganza going on nearby, as we could hear loud chanting, singing and frenetic preaching booming out over a high-powered public address system. We went to bed, but the noise continued till 3.30 in the morning, and of course at 6 o'clock we had the chickens waking us up again.

By then we had a pretty good daily routine established. We would walk down the hill past our friends at the recycling centre to get to the office about 8 o'clock. Most days we would get some kind of lunch at work, usually involving banku or fufu. We would leave about 4 or 5 o'clock and walk back up the hill to the flat, arriving hot and sweaty. After a shower we would sit out on the balcony with our 'sundowners'.

After sunset we cooked dinner on our gas rings, and sat outside again over coffee. For entertainment we read or watched the TV. There was a single channel which we watched, as the others were either in local languages or just sport. 'Joy TV' normally showed a film at 9 pm, and we would sit down and decide if it worth watching – provided there was power. Otherwise, we would watch a DVD on the laptop, often a Poirot mystery from the set we had brought out with us. We would go to bed about midnight, or earlier if there was no power, ready for the sun and chickens to wake us again at 6 o'clock next morning.

The Ongoing Omega Saga

While we were settling into life at home, at work there were still many challenges to face. The feedback we had produced at the end of the previous term had gone out to teachers and school managers, although it was not complete. For the teachers we had produced the following for the class that they taught:

1. A table showing the scores achieved by each student in English, mathematics and science and whether they were significantly above, below or at the class average for that subject. The feedback also highlighted students who were below average in all three subjects, as well as those above average in all three.
2. A table for each subject, showing for each item (question) whether a student got it right or wrong. It also showed items where a student got the item wrong unexpectedly, based on the difficulty of the item and the student's overall score in the subject.
3. A table for each subject, showing the percentage getting each item right or wrong, with a brief summary of the question content and the overall percentage getting it right (also known as the 'facility').

The idea was that Table 1 would show the subjects in which individual students were strong or weak, compared with their peers, as well as those students who were struggling in all subjects or needed extra challenge as they were ahead of their peers in every subject.

We were keen not to give teachers any information which would compare their students' performance with those in other schools, as we were concerned that this would make them afraid for their jobs if they were under-performing, and might encourage them to cheat. We were aware that this was an issue for some teachers, however much we emphasised that the tests and feedback were to help them improve their students' learning, not to judge or condemn their teaching.

Table 2 was intended to highlight particular areas of each subject where individual students might be weak, and where remedial help might be needed. Table 3, on the other hand, was designed to show subject areas which were poorly understood by the class as a whole, and where further teaching would be helpful.

In addition to the tables, the feedback booklets contained copious notes about how to interpret and use them to improve teaching and learning for the future. The questions we now had to answer were: did the teachers understand the feedback? Were they using the information in their teaching? Which elements did they find most useful? Was there anything we could add which would be helpful?

In addition to feedback for teachers, we had produced some for the school managers, the administrative heads of each of the ten schools. In this case, we wanted them to be able to compare their school's results for each subject in each year with those of all other Omega schools. To do this we computed 'Omega scores' for each subject each year, which were the original 'raw' test scores rescaled to have a fixed average of 50 across all students, with a fixed standard deviation of 10. This meant that Omega scores all ranged from 20 to 80, and those under 50 were below average and those over 50 above average.

We presented the average Omega scores for each school in different ways, in graphs and tables, so that the school managers could see how each year group stacked up in every subject compared with the overall results. A detailed example of all the feedback is given in Appendix A, together with the explanatory notes that went with it.

Our first task on returning to Ghana after Christmas was to interview all the teachers and school managers about the feedback they had received, to try to answer the questions set out above. This meant us touring all the schools by taxi, with my colleague Ato as minder. We managed two or three schools a day, though sometimes with difficulty. One of the main problems was finding our way to every school, even with Ato's help, as some of the Omega schools are well off the beaten track.

At each school Sandie interviewed the school managers while Ato and I talked to the teachers in a group and then spoke to each one individually. After we had finished all the schools we compared notes and wrote a brief report which we shared with Ken, and James when he arrived later.

From our interviews we got some comments and suggestions which allowed us to modify the feedback slightly, and improve elements that were less well understood. However, I believe we also ran into a problem which is common in Ghana, and possibly in Africa overall. People are lovely and friendly, but have a tendency to tell you what they think you want to hear. They praised the feedback and said it was useful and they were using it in their teaching, but it was hard to get much firm evidence that this was the case. Our main hope was that as time went by they would get more familiar with what we were producing and find it increasingly useful in their teaching.

Just as we were finishing off these interviews, we had arranged a workshop on assessment for the Omega subject specialists, who were responsible for developing the mid-term tests and the end of term exams. We wanted to give them some guidance on test development, in an effort to improve the quality of the assessments and their usefulness in guiding future teaching.

We and all the subject specialists got in one of the school buses and drove to a business centre near Weija Junction, and had a two–hour session there. We had developed a dummy test with a combination of items from  the recent mid-terms, and got the subject specialists to find problems with these items. Afterwards we discussed these problems and developed some guidelines for producing better items in future. We felt the workshop had gone well, though again the proof would only lie in a perceptible improvement in test quality.

Test development seminar

When we got back to the Oblogo office we found that two new laptops had been delivered for us to use. This was a big improvement for us, as the PCs we had been using crashed as soon as the power fluctuated slightly, and could not be used at all when the power was off. The laptops ran off batteries, which were charged when the electricity was on, and could therefore be used for several hours even in a power cut.

The next day James arrived, and we had a long meeting with him, discussing how things were going. In the afternoon we went with him to the Crown Liberty Hotel, on top of a hill on the road to Kokrobite. This is quite smart, though there did not seem to be many people about. We had a meal with him next to the pool, and then we got a taxi to take him back to his hotel and us back home.

The day after that, we turned up as usual at the office, to find it all locked up and no sign of life at the school. We waited for over half an hour before Ken came to let us in. It seemed there was a big funeral in Oblogo today and they were worried about trouble, so had given the kids a day off. We worked on our laptops, and in the afternoon there was an education team meeting which James addressed.

We avoided Oblogo on the way home, but then detoured over to the main dirt road up the hill to get some fruit. They had begun to dig a massive ditch by the side of the road, so we had to do a further detour to get home. The digging of this ditch went on for months, and apparently the government had funded it to provide drainage of rain water from the top of the hill. The work made the dirt road, the only access to Gbawe Top Base, even worse than usual, and we wondered if the money would not have been better spent improving the road.

The ditch

When the ditch was finished it ran from the top of the hill to the bottom, by Oblogo, and was lined with concrete. Businesses on that side of the road had to install wobbly plank bridges so their customers could reach them. However, there was a dip in the road near the top, so the water all flowed into that dip and created a large muddy pool, and almost no water ran down to the bottom. It struck us as a poorly planned and pointless exercise, although it must have created jobs for a number of workers.

On the last Friday in January there was a rather rowdy education team meeting, in which James harangued the staff about their lack of dedication and commitment. After he left a row broke out between some of the people there, so we sloped off back to our office. Meanwhile, I was struggling to get data to do feedback, and also finding the quality of the data I did receive quite poor.

One of the problems was tracking pupils – I had tried to assign each pupil a unique identifying number which would be carried through from subject to subject and year to year. In some cases, however, teachers were allocating their own numbers, and in others it was obvious that the same number was being given to different students.

As mentioned previously, the main issue was the somewhat random way that Ghanaian pupils wrote their names. Apart from spelling variations, they would switch round the order, so that 'Gifty Bright' on one test paper would be 'Bright Gifty' on another. They might also have an alternate surname or middle name, so that 'Gifty Bright' could well be the same person as 'Gifty Ofuso'. This could make matching up students' test scripts and scores a positive nightmare.

The solution I came up with was to use the data I already had about pupils from earlier tests, and create exhaustive class lists for the teachers to look at, and mark where two apparently different pupils were the same, and write in the names of new pupils to be allocated unique numbers. I printed these out, and handed them to Ato and Andrew to take round the schools, together with a sheet of instructions to the teachers about what to do with them.

Eventually these class lists began to trickle back, and in some cases they had been filled in correctly and were really useful. In other cases, the teachers had failed to understand the instructions and they were less helpful, but I was beginning to realise that this was normal. We would have to explore other solutions to the whole range of data entry issues.

A few days later things were made more awkward when the office generator had a sudden massive power surge which blew out both our laptop chargers and the light bulb in our room. Fortunately, we had a spare charger which we were able to share until such time as another one could be provided.

Meanwhile, Sandie was being kept busy quality assuring some of the teaching materials which were coming in from Ghanaian consultants to be used in various subjects, including English, mathematics and science. In many cases she had her work cut out trying to turn these into something which could be sensibly used for teaching. As well as basic English mistakes, she was able to detect fundamental errors in some of the mathematics and science materials, despite being an expert in neither subject!

In the first two months of 2012 we felt that we had made some progress in our work with Omega Schools, but there was clearly still a lot to be done.

Cape Coast again

Soon after our arrival we returned to Cape Coast. This time Ato and his friend Nana were going there by bus from Accra, so they went off in mid-afternoon to buy tickets for the four of us, saying the bus would stop at Weija Junction to pick us up. We went down there at 4 o'clock and waited, and later got a text from Ato saying the bus was running late. Nearby was a 'spot' (a local basic bar), so we sat there with a couple of drinks and waited.

Finally the bus arrived at 6 o'clock and picked us up. It was quite luxurious, but the main problem was the air conditioning, which was turned up to the extreme and blasted freezing air at us, so we were shivering with cold. We were eventually dropped off on the outskirts of Cape Coast, and got a taxi to the Prospect Lodge once more.

We checked in and were given a 'queen room' on the top floor, which unfortunately had no water. We went and told this to reception, and they promised someone would turn the pump on, so we went out on the terrace to have a meal. The service was shocking, with a waitress who didn't seem to have a clue. We had to wait an hour for food. When it came, Sandie's vegetable plate had a great lump of chicken on it!

Catholic cathedral

After the usual 40-minute wait for breakfast next morning, we went out to explore the town. On the other side of Cape Coast, past the Might Victory Hotel, is Fort Victoria. We paid to have a guide take us up there. It is a small fort, with four cannons, and to get inside we had to climb up a rusty iron ladder. There was a good view from the top, though it was very hazy, but the guide insisted on pointing out to us almost every building in town, which got a bit wearing but must have been how he earned his money.

From there we passed the big catholic cathedral. There was obviously something going on, as a crowd of smartly-dressed people was waiting

Fort William

outside. Apparently there were three funerals happening at the same time, and these were some of the mourners. Fort William stands on top of another hill, up a rough path. Here we were shown round by someone who apparently lived there with his family, but was much more taciturn than our previous guide. This fort is bigger, with more cannons, and has a lighthouse in the middle.

For lunch we returned to the Baobab café, and in the shop there Sandie bought a local dress with a lively pattern. We rested in the hotel for a couple of hours, and then went down to the beach resort. We had drinks and walked along the beach. It was murky and hazy, and we were not tempted to go in the sea. After cocktails by the beach, we went to the Castle restaurant nearby for dinner.

We ordered a bottle of red wine, and the waiter brought a few bottles for us to choose from, in a kind of milk crate. This is normal practice in Ghanaian restaurants, which tend not to have a wine list. It was quite dark in there, so we picked one at random – but when we began to drink it we found it was very sweet and pretty disgusting. A careful examination of

57

the label by the light of a mobile phone revealed that the wine came from Brazil, which explained why it was so sweet. Our time in Brazil the previous year had made it clear that Brazilian wines are all much too sweet and quite undrinkable. This was one of the few times when we left a bottle of wine more than half full when we finished our meal. Why anyone would import Brazilian wines remains a mystery to us.

On Sunday we took a tro-tro over some pretty rough roads to Kakum National Park. Once there we booked up for a canopy walk and a ground-level nature walk. We chickened out of the canopy walk early on, because the walkway was pretty high and swayed alarmingly, especially with a number of people on it. The nature walk took us through the forest, but there was little in the way of wildlife to see, apart from a green mamba curled up in a tree and some brightly-coloured lizards. Another tro-tro took us back to Cape Coast, where we got a rather cramped Metro Mass bus back to Weija Junction.

Kakum lizard

Fete

James had recommended a beach resort at Fete, on the coast west of Accra, so on the first Saturday in February we set off there for a weekend break. We got tro-tros to Kasoa, and then a long-distance tro-tro to Awutu Beraku, where we found a taxi to take us down to Till's No. 1 Beach Resort. We checked in, and found the place was actually quite smart. The morning was spent relaxing on the beach, though the sea had the usual complement of black plastic bags. The resort was quiet, with only a few people, mainly white, staying there.

It all changed after lunch. Suddenly about three coachloads of people arrived, and they swarmed over the resort and the beach. It was obviously some kind of outing, perhaps from a local church. They were good natured and clearly enjoying themselves, but the transformation was quite startling. The visitors stayed for the afternoon and then left again at 6 o'clock.

We had a walk along the beach and found lots of shells, as well as the remains of another beach resort which had clearly been abandoned and left to decay. Perhaps it was Till's No. 2. Dinner was in an open circular restaurant with a thatched roof, with good food, poor wine and indifferent service.

On Sunday, after a nice breakfast, we walked into Fete, passing a number of giant termite mounds. From there a shared taxi took us to the larger coastal town of Senya Beraku. Like many of the coastal towns, this is dominated by an old fort, now a hostel, and from the battlements there are good views along the coast. After admiring the colourful fishing boats on the beach, we returned to Fete and the hotel, and chilled out there till about 2 o'clock. A taxi from Fete took us back to the coast road, where we got a tro-tro to Kasoa and another back to Weija Junction.

Termite mound

Senya Beraka fort

Abandze

Two weeks later we travelled further along the coast road to Abandze Beach Resort. Though not quite as smart as the one at Fete, we had a nice

Abandze Beach Resort

two-room chalet with a thatched roof and a veranda. We had lunch on the beach and watched the waves breaking spectacularly on the rocks just offshore. Later we went for a walk along the beach towards Fort Amsterdam, another old coastal defence on a nearby headland. The beach route was obstructed by boats,

so we cut back to the main road, and then through the village and up a flight of steps to the fort.

Fort Amsterdam

Although quite impressive, the fort itself had no-one looking after it and thus no admission fee, and we could just walk in. The downside was a bunch of children who followed us about and continually pestered us for money – quite unusual, in our experience in Ghana. After looking inside, we went to walk round the

outside, but these kids were such a nuisance we soon gave up.

After a quick walk down to the beach, where the adults pestered us as well, we returned to the resort by the main road. Evening drinks were in an upstairs lounge overlooking the beach, and the owner, a Scotswoman called Susan, came to chat to us. Apparently she came out to Ghana on holiday, decided she liked the area, and bought the resort – possibly some kind of record for impulse purchasing. Dinner was served by the light of hurricane lamps, and the food was good. Unfortunately the waiter announced that they had run out of wine, but then Susan came round and offered us some from her own supply, so Mafeking was relieved.

Obrunni!

On Sunday we checked out and walked up the road to the nearby town of Saltpond. There was quite an elaborate posuban shrine there, but one of the locals sternly forbade us to take pictures of it. A sudden rainstorm forced us to shelter under a tree, and afterwards we looked at the large church and smart mosque in the town before getting a tro-tro into Cape Coast. From there we got the Metro Mass bus back to Weija Junction.

A short break in England

Having discovered the 60-day rule relating to our visas, we had carefully timed our next flight home to get us out of the country again before we fell foul of it. Our taxi driver Alex picked us up in the afternoon of the 29th February and drove us into Accra. The trip was amazingly smooth, as they had finally finished all the road works and built the shiny new bypass around Accra. This rejoiced in the name of 'George W. Bush Highway', as it was funded by the USA.

He dropped us at the Western Sun Hotel again and we chilled out there and had a meal, before getting the shuttle to the airport. There was the usual chaos in the terminal, but once on the plane the flight was smooth and uneventful, and brought us back to Terminal 5 at 6 o'clock in the morning. Claire came and picked us up, and dropped us at the Travelodge in Wycombe.

During our brief visit to England, we stayed for a few days in Sheringham, Norfolk with Claire and her two young sons. While there we attended the 40th wedding anniversary celebrations of our friends Linda and Donnie, held near Great Yarmouth – Sandie's home town. On the way back we visited our son Andrew and his family, in Faversham, Kent, before returning to Wycombe, ready to fly back to Ghana the next day.

Obrunni!

Chapter 6: Exploring Ghana

Home Again

The flat in Ghana was the only home we had at this stage, so in many ways we were glad to be back in our own place. The flight was uneventful, except that at Terminal 5 our laptop suddenly froze up and refused to do anything. When we landed at Accra Alex with his smiling face was there to welcome us, and drive us home. The trip was amazingly fast, because of the brand-new road system around Accra.

At home, we discovered that the problem with the tank had been fixed, and we unloaded all the stuff we had brought back with us: food, DVDs, painting gear for me, kitchen equipment and so forth. The day after landing we went down to the office and greeted all our friends there, and handed over the dead laptop to Eddie the IT guru. Two days later he handed it back in working order, saying he had dismantled it and cleaned it out, and we expressed our gratitude.

'Bra lady' at Oblogo

Life at Gbawe Top Base soon settled into our usual routine. We went to work, came back and had a shower, followed by sunset drinks on the terrace. Sometimes we went to the local shops to buy gin, tonic, beer, water, phone top-up or other essentials of life. Local kids still called out 'Obrunni!' when they saw us, although by now we must have been a common sight wandering around the neighbourhood.

The Sizzler restaurant became our local venue for a night out. We would walk down the hill and get a tro-tro to Shoprite to pick up supplies, and then walk back along the main road to the Sizzler, where I would get my lobster and chips and we would indulge in a bottle of (non-Brazilian) wine. Alex would be summoned with his taxi to pick us up afterwards and take us home. On

Sundays we would frequently go to Kokrobite beach for rest and relaxation, always ending with cocktails at Big Milly's.

One weekend in March we rang Big Milly's and managed to book a room for the Saturday night. It was a pretty basic en-suite, but meant we could stay into the evening. In the afternoon we had a drink at their bar, and sat there watching the world's smallest lizard sipping the condensation from Sandie's beer bottle. In the evening there was loud reggae music, which improved markedly once they switched to playing Bob Marley classics.

Kokrobite Beach, and the tiny lizard

On Sunday we went round to the nearby Kokrobite Garden restaurant, which was run by an Italian-Spanish couple. They did excellent pizzas for lunch, as well as genuine cappuccinos. Having discovered this, it became one of our favourite places to visit each time we went to the beach, and we got to know the two young people who ran it pretty well.

On the last Saturday in March we made another trip into Accra, continuing our exploration of the sprawling capital city. One place we visited was the Nkrumah Gardens and Mausoleum, near the sea. The place is well-kept and interesting, with a giant edifice in the middle, water features with statues and fountains, and loads of wedding parties having their photos taken.

Nkrumah Gardens

Wedding party

Our next mission was to find a seafront bar we had seen advertised, and eventually we reached the Osekan bar, right by the sea with waves crashing over rocks nearby. We stayed for a drink, followed by a meal and bottle of wine, and then a taxi home.

On subsequent excursions to Accra we visited the so-called 'Oxford Street' area and found the Koala supermarket, which specialised in imported goods for expatriates at inflated prices, as well as Ryan's Irish pub, which did an excellent line in fish and chips. On another Saturday we saw Independence Square, a big Stalinist arch with attached parade ground where they have major national celebrations, and had a meal in the Tribes restaurant of the Afia Beach Resort.

Omega challenges and triumphs

Meanwhile, the work at Omega Schools continued with many challenges, some disasters and a few successes. I returned somewhat hopeful that all the data from last term would be waiting for me to analyse, but was less than astonished when it was not.

The next day some of the data that had been scanned in began to arrive, so I started the task of converting it from Word format to Excel, so that it could be entered as data into the statistical package SPSS for analysis. The data continued to trickle in over the next few days, and after we had been there about a week James Tooley arrived back in Ghana. He announced with great excitement that he had managed to negotiate a sponsorship deal with the Pearson organisation. In the afternoon we all had biscuits and fizzy drink to celebrate.

The following day Sandie was invited to attend a 'literacy extravaganza' at one of the schools, so she went off with James for most of the day. When they came back, James insisted on going with us to Daddy's Cottage at Weija, despite the fact that he was feeling unwell.

Dinner at Big Milly's

A day or two later a group of about ten students from Newcastle University came out to find out about Omega Schools. We were invited to join them for a meal at Big Milly's on Kokrobite Beach one evening. We had a pleasant time together, and after they left we stayed for another drink, waiting for our taxi driver Alex to come and take us home.

Back at the office, I had finally got all the test data I was likely to get, and had converted it to Excel and fed it through my programs to generate school and teacher feedback. After printing and carefully collating it, Sandie sent it off to be bound into reports for each school and class. We both got extremely frustrated when it returned, because it came back wrongly collated and bound, and the whole thing had to be done again.

We carried on frantically generating feedback reports, and then heard that James had been taken off to hospital with malaria. Apparently, because he spent so much time in malaria-infested areas, he did not bother with taking preventative medication, as we did religiously. He emerged from hospital the next day, but phoned to say he was still weak and flying home. So on the day of the great feedback presentation, we had to manage without him.

Discussing the feedback

The following day was the meeting with teachers and school managers to discuss the feedback and hand it out. The fact that we had managed to produce it in time was the major triumph to date. It was held at the big half-built church which Ken attended, behind Shoprite. Teachers and school managers arrived from all over in dribs and drabs, and we gave them their reports as they showed up. We did a presentation on what the reports meant, how to read them, and how to use the information to guide their future teaching. There were then discussion groups, but it was hard to get people to focus on the reports and their content.

After the meeting we walked down the road to a bar for well-earned drinks, with extremely loud muzak. We were pleased with the reports we had managed to produce, but unsure what impact they would actually have on teaching and learning.

A few days later we learned that there was a school managers' meeting in the afternoon at Kasoa 94 school, and that this would be good opportunity to hand out their feedback reports. We got a taxi there, but the taxi driver got a bit lost. When we finally arrived, we were the first ones there. When the school managers showed up, we handed out the reports for their schools and explained what they meant and how to use them. There was also some group work afterwards. After the meeting we walked to the main road through the Muslim section of Kasoa, and caught a taxi.

It was now the Easter holidays, and having (mostly) achieved our goal of getting feedback reports produced and given out, we felt we deserved a short break, and it was time to explore some other parts of Ghana. With that in mind, we set off on a ten-day tour, starting at Kumasi in the centre of the country and then travelling up to the northern regions.

Off to Kumasi

We had booked a tour with a car and driver of the northern regions of Ghana, starting in Kumasi, but first we had to get there. We had found a company called VIP that ran buses from Accra to Kumasi, so set off on Friday 6th April on the first leg of our travels. Alex picked us up early to take us to the bus station, but unfortunately on the way his car developed a flat tyre. This is not an unusual occurrence, given the state of many of the roads and the quality of the tyres. He stopped by the road to change the wheel, handicapped by the fact that his jack was too big for the car.

Eventually we set off again, and reached the bus station. Sandie bought tickets and we found the bus, put the case in the hold and got on. It was quite luxurious, with plenty of legroom, a/c that was not too fierce and a TV that played African DVDs all the way. We set off at 8.45 and the journey took 6 hours, mainly because of the really poor condition of the roads. We stopped briefly at a rest area halfway but did not have a lot of time there. Finally, we arrived in Kumasi just before 3 pm.

Kumasi is the second largest city in the country, centre of the Ashanti region, so we were baffled as to why the road between it and Accra was so bad, especially compared with the Coast Road and the highways round Accra. We were informed that the politicians in Accra wanted to keep Kumasi in its second-rate status and therefore had vetoed any road improvement. How true this is, we do not know.

A taxi driver approached us, and promised to take us to the Four Villages Inn, where we had booked accommodation for three nights. The only snag was that he did not have a clue where it was. We tried to show him in the guidebook, but he kept stopping at other hotels to ask the way. Eventually, after a long detour, we arrived at the hotel, several miles south of the town centre. We checked in and were shown our room. This was fine, but not outstanding, and the whole place seemed expensive.

After having a shower and some tea, we went back into the town. A shared taxi took us to the ring road, and another taxi to the centre. Our walk round the town took us past a red fort with military hardware lined up outside, and a couple of roundabouts with statues in the middle. One quite impressive one showed a lion with a man standing on its back.

Kumasi statue

After our circuit we reached Victor Baidoo's, a café recommended in the guidebook. We had drinks first – I managed to get a G&T – and later ordered veggie burgers. They had an extensive menu, and the food was OK, but it got very crowded and the a/c was quite fierce. We got a taxi back to the hotel, and sat out on the verandah for a bit with coffee and fruit.

We chatted to some of the other guests over breakfast at 8 o'clock, and afterwards Chris, the owner of the hotel, took us for the 'tour' we had booked with him to Lake Bosontwe. He drove us out of town to the south-west and down towards the lake. We had to stop at a barrier and pay to go on, and then descended the crater rim towards the lake (which is an old meteor crater). Chris drove down to the main lakeside village and then on to the Lake Bosontwe Paradise resort, where he left us, arranging to pick us up later. We decided to go for a walk, and followed the lakeside dirt road on to the next village and beyond, with some good views of the lake.

Lake Bosontwe

Back at the resort, we decided to go out in their canoe, but were told there were pedaloes back at the village. One of the staff took us round there, where it was all happening, with bars and people and swimming. He negotiated a pedalo for us to take out for half an hour. We cruised about for a bit, getting views from the water. Then we returned to the resort, and had a drink while waiting for Chris to take us back.

After tea/coffee and snacks, we got changed and headed back to the town. We got a shared taxi to the centre and some more cash from an ATM, and then headed up to the enormous market. The streets near the market were crowded with people, stalls and traffic. The market itself was extremely busy. We walked through and managed to emerge on the other side. Our next goal was the Maniya Palace, which was supposed to be nearby. After wandering along several streets and asking a few times, we found it eventually. At the entrance near the museum there were a number of peacocks. After walking round the outside of the compound we reached the main entrance, though it was not possible to get into the palace itself.

Back at the centre of town, we made our way to the Eclipse bar, where we collapsed in a heap with drinks, watching the world and the traffic go by. That was fine for a while, and then they turned on a deafening noise machine which drove us away fairly soon. We went looking for a restaurant, but struggled to find one that was open and not deafeningly noisy. Finally, we got a taxi to the Royal Park Hotel, which has a Chinese restaurant. We had a decent meal there and then a last taxi back to the hotel.

Besease Ashanti shrine

The next day, after getting a shared taxi up to the town, we caught a tro-tro to Ejisu, on the road back to Accra. From there we got a taxi to Besease, where there is an ancient Ashanti shrine which is now a museum. We went in and were greeted by an old man who welcomed us and allowed us to look round. The place was interesting, with lots of unusual symbols on the wall, but quite run down.

From there we walked back a bit and got a shared taxi back towards Ejisu, getting off at a drinking spot just before the town. Having studied the guidebook over a drink, we decided to go to Adanwomase. We walked back to the town and got a taxi to take us to this little village with a community tourist venture. When we got there the visitor centre was shut, but we waited while some women phoned for someone, who turned up fairly soon. His name was Eric, and he did us the combined tour of kente weaving and the village.

Kente cloth

He showed us the technique of making kente cloth, and took us to the weaving centre where I had a go but was very slow – not very likely to make a career at kente weaving. Afterwards we visited the cocoa plantation and saw cocoa beans growing. Eric also took us to a couple of village stores, and we bought a tie and purse in kente fabric. His nephew took us to see the sacred tree and the chief's palace, and after all that we waited for a tro-tro back to Kumasi.

It came at last and we piled in. It took over an hour to Kumasi, and eventually dropped us at the bus station in the north of the town. We walked through the town, which was fairly quiet, and had drinks again at the Eclipse bar. Afterwards we looked at the Presbyterian church and bought some apples before getting a shared taxi back to the hotel. The weather turned stormy and it began to rain.

Chris drove us up the road to the Relax restaurant, which does Chinese and Indian food. We had some tasty Indian food there, and by the time the meal was over it had stopped raining. We got a taxi back to the hotel for our last night there.

Northward Ho!

On Monday morning we sat on the verandah, waiting for our driver Ahmed, who was supposed to pick us up at 10 am. At 11 o'clock we rang him, to discover he did not know where the hotel was. He finally arrived at 11.15, and we piled into his 4x4 vehicle with our luggage. He headed out of Kumasi, fairly slowly because of the traffic, and took the road towards Tamale. We drove for about 2½ hours to reach the Kintampo Falls Park, where Ahmed left us while he went to get himself some lunch.

Kintampo Falls

The place was absolutely heaving with a Bank Holiday Monday crowd. We paid to get into the park, and followed the circular walk which led past a couple of small waterfalls to the big one. There were 152 steps, packed with people going up and down. At the bottom people were jammed into the pool below the falls or climbing up the falls themselves. We took some photos and fought our way back up to the top again. I bought a drink, and we went outside and waited for Ahmed.

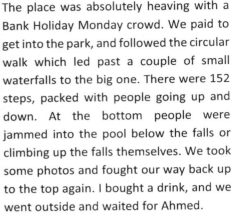

Tamale Mosque

The road to Tamale got a bit rougher as we approached the city. We eventually got there about 5.30, and checked into the Picorna hotel, with a fairly small and pokey room. We changed quickly and went out, walking along the road past a market, the large mosque and the palace (a collection of red mud huts with thatched roofs).

There was a noticeable difference now between this town and those further south, in particular the sense that we were in a predominantly Muslim area, as well as one which was more traditional in its culture. We began working our way through the ATMs we passed, trying to get cash out, but tried a number with no success. Finally, I got some money out from one ATM with my UK bank card.

After this success we went to the Crest restaurant (recommended in the guidebook) to have a meal. This had a roof terrace which was pitch dark and very noisy, so we went in the actual restaurant downstairs. We ended up sitting on the balcony, which was quite pleasant. The food was quite good (I had fish and chips), though the drinks were very limited and there was no coffee.

Back at the hotel there was a loud disco going on near our room. One of the staff came along and offered to change it for a different room, to which we gladly agreed. The new room was much quieter and more spacious, though the electrical sockets did not work. Eventually they brought us a couple of extension leads which brought in power from outside, and we managed like that. About 3.30 am we heard a noise of dripping water from just outside, and there was clearly a big leak from up above somewhere which carried on till the morning. We managed to get back to sleep, however.

In the morning, after breakfast, Ahmed was waiting for us. He took us on a very brief tour of Tamale, including the smart new football stadium, and then took us to the STC bus station, where we bought tickets back to Kumasi for Saturday, five days hence. He headed north towards Bolgatanga, and after about 1½ hours we reached the Tongo Rocks visitor centre, a little shack with no-one around. Eventually we found someone who agreed to take us on a tour.

Tongo village is surrounded by massive piles of rocks, and our tour took us to visit 'caves' within several of these. First we went to the 'school cave', an overhang which served as a primary school until about ten years previously.

Tongo Rocks

Then we went to the 'Hiding cave', where the locals used to hide from the British, and where with a bit of a scramble we were able to penetrate deep into the pile of rocks. Next we visited the 'Hyena cave', a broad expanse with a flat floor but a low ceiling, where the hyenas used to lurk. After that the guide spent a bit of time chatting to his mates, and then took us to see the chief's house and the tombs of former chiefs before returning us to the start.

From there we drove back to the main road and up to Bolgatanga, where Ahmed dropped us at a restaurant called 'Comme ci comme ca', supposedly the best in north Ghana. The place was very smartly decorated, and the drinks came quickly enough, but we had to wait at least 45 minutes for some sandwiches.

Crocodiles and hippos

Our next stop was at Paga, on the border with Burkina Faso, where we visited one of the famous 'crocodile ponds', originally kept by the chiefs up there as a kind of status symbol. It was basically a pond full of Nile crocodiles, who all seemed very bored and harmless.

Paga crocodile

We did not stay long there, but drove back to the Pikworo slave camp, a local ecotourism project. This where, back in the past, slaves captured inland were kept before being sold to the British or Butch slave traders on the coast. A guide showed us round another group of rocks, explaining how the slaves used to eat in one place and be entertained in another. At

this point a number of locals began drumming on the rocks while a group of children jigged about, to illustrate what he was saying. Needless to say, we had to give them a 'donation'. We also went to a lookout point, a slave cemetery, and a 'punishment rock' where

Entertainment at Pikworo

recalcitrant slaves were chained till they died of exposure.

The next stop was Navrongo and the large mud-built Catholic cathedral. Inside there were some interesting pillar decorations, but not much else. After that we were taken to our nearby hotel, the Mayaga. This was quite smartly finished outside, and the room was spacious, but there was no hot water in the shower. After changing we had drinks in the rear courtyard – I had an interesting aniseed liquor instead of the gin I'd ordered, with Sprite. Later we had dinner out there – rice and veg for Sandie, rice and fish for me. A skinny cat came and begged for the fish after I'd finished it, and probably got more from it than I did. One success was that they managed to bring us coffee afterwards.

In the morning we persuaded Ahmed to return to Paga to let us look at Paga Pia's palace. This is a rambling mud structure with some interesting decorations out front, including bricks in the shape of crocodiles. We were shown round, including into a 'safety room' with a very low entrance, so you can strike intruders on the head as they bend to get in. Otherwise, it was not particularly exciting.

At Page Pia's palace

Wa mosque

We drove back to Navrongo and took the road to Wa, which is unsealed most of the way. Ahmed took it at a fair pace, so we had a rather bumpy ride. On arrival in Wa we had a look at the outside of an old palace and a couple of mosques, and then went round to our hotel, the Teegber Catholic Guesthouse. We dumped our bags and went to have lunch in the restaurant, where we had some decent chips.

Afterwards Ahmed collected us and drove us down to the Wechiau Hippo sanctuary. We picked up a guide and then a paddler and some lifejackets on the rough track down to the river. There we got into a wooden canoe with a number of leaky joints and set off, with the guide furiously bailing. We paddled down the Black Volta for a bit till we spotted two groups of hippos in the water, and pulled into the Burkina Faso shore to take film and photos of them. They did not do much, except that one of them gave a prodigious yawn. After we had taken enough photos we gave the signal to return to the start, and stepped ashore, relieved that the canoe had got us there and back without sinking. It was also good that we had encountered the most dangerous animals in Africa in their natural habitat without any unfortunate incident.

Hippos on the Black Volta

Mole National Park

Larabanga Mosque

The next morning we drove out of Wa and down the road to Mole National Park, which took over two hours. We stopped at Larabanga, at the park entrance, to see the ancient mosque there. This is quite unusual, being built of mud with sticks thrust through it, and we took a number of photos.

Waterhole at Mole

From there we drove into the park and checked into the Mole Motel. This has a swimming pool and a lookout over a couple of waterholes where animals come to drink. We spent a fair bit of time by the pool, having lunch and the occasional swim, sitting under an umbrella at a table by the pool. At 3 o'clock we changed and got ready for our driving safari.

Ahmed took us in his car, together with a ranger with a gun. We saw baboons and warthogs near the accommodation, and later saw a couple of different types of antelope. We also saw a group of elephants, but they rushed into the bush as we approached. We drove around for a while more, without seeing much else, and then returned to the motel.

Mole wildlife

We found the water was off when we returned, so we changed and went back to the poolside for drinks. Later on I checked and found the water was running, so I was able to have a shower. We got some wine and had a meal by the pool. During the night there was a heavy storm which battered on the roof of our room.

When we got up the next morning we discovered there were two large puddles in the room, and one of them was round Sandie's camera bag. Fortunately her camera and our passports were OK, but some of the banknotes were damp and her notebook was very wet.

Elephant crossing

We set off early for a guided walk, starting at 7 am. We were in a big group with a number of Canadian nurses, who were volunteering at hospitals in Ghana and having a tour of the north over Easter, like us. Soon after setting out we found a couple of elephants near the staff lodgings, and tracked them through the bush till we were able to see them crossing a road. We carried on trekking through the bush, with our shoes getting pretty muddy, till we reached the further of the two waterholes. We went back to the near waterhole and then climbed up the hill to the motel.

Canoe excursion

After that it was breakfast time, and we spent a few hours sitting by the pool with drinks, reading and doing Sudoku. After lunch (chips), Ahmed appeared and said we should go on the canoe safari soon, so we got ready. He drove us to the village of Mognori, where we picked up a guide and couple of paddlers, and then went down to the river. We were paddled up the river in another leaky canoe, with not much to see except some brightly coloured kingfishers. The river was narrow, with trees arching overhead, and the whole trip lasted about 40 minutes.

Obrunni!

On our return to the motel we spent a little time in the gift shop, buying souvenirs. Then back to the poolside and our evening drinks, and watching the sun go down, to the sound of crazy Canadians diving into the pool. Back in the room we waited for the water to come on so we could have a shower. At 7.30 we returned to the poolside with the other half of our bottle of wine to have a pleasant meal under the stars, followed by an early night.

Return to Kumasi

We set the alarms for 3 am and got up in the dark, then packed and went round to the car to wait for Ahmed. Eventually I had to go and rouse him from his dorm. We set off at about 3.45, driving along a bumpy unsealed road in the dark, which was not a lot of fun. Every village we came to had goats sleeping in the road, who had to scatter as we came along. Eventually we reached the main road and it got lighter, and we reached Tamale STC station about 6 am. We said goodbye to Ahmed and waited for our bus to board. Sandie went and got some tasty fried quasi-doughnuts for breakfast.

The bus set off soon after 7 am, and the journey took about 6 hours with a break at Kintampo for some disgusting toilets. During the whole trip there were weird African soaps on the TV. We reached Kumasi soon after 1 pm, and walked through the town to the Sanbra hotel.

After checking in we went out to visit the fort, and had a guided tour of the military museum there, which was not very exciting. Afterwards we walked up the road to the hospital. This has a building in the grounds which houses the Ashanti sword – a kind of local version of Excalibur. Needless to say, the building was closed. The cultural centre was closed as well, so it was not an entirely successful excursion.

We walked round to the Eclipse bar for our usual evening drinks. The girl there recognised us and brought our drinks without being asked. About 6.30 we went back to the hotel, and later to the hotel restaurant for a meal to celebrate Sandie's birthday. The food was good, and we had a nice bottle of Shiraz – the portions were enormous, but the service poor.

79

Obrunni!

After a late start the next morning, we walked up past the zoo, looking for an advertised bat colony. We saw the bats flying among the trees, but never found a way in to the place where they were. From there we walked back through the market and found the road up to the palace, in order to see the six-weekly 'Adae Festival', at which local chiefs honour the Ashanti king. We arrived soon after 10 o'clock, which was when we had been told things would start, but there was no sign of anything happening. We sat under a tree for a bit, and then got chatting to a Dutch couple and had a drink with them in a nearby bar (fruit juice only). At about 11.30 we went through a gateway to the place where the ceremony was to be held, and were given seats in the front row under an awning.

We waited till about 12.15, as more and more of the locals arrived to take part, dressed in their colourful local costume, draped in kente cloth – and talking on their mobile phones. Then the drums started and the king with his retinue came in procession, which was quite picturesque. There was a group of people with long horns, another group with drums, some with muskets and an individual carrying the king's special chair.

Adae Festival at Kumasi

There was then a long period with people being presented and offering homage, which was less exciting. We finally quit about 1.40 and got a taxi back to the hotel, where we picked up our luggage. Then the taxi took us to the VIP bus station where we bought tickets and got on the bus, which left about ten minutes later.

The journey was mostly uneventful. After nearly three hours we stopped at the rest area, and bought some food (fish pie and coke for me). The next part of the journey was on the very rough unfinished road, and quite slow. We stopped to pick up some passengers from a broken-down bus, and they all sat in the aisle. Eventually we reached the bus station at Accra about 7.45, and Alex came to pick us up five minutes later.

When we reached home we felt we had a much better idea of the variety of this country in which we were spending a year. At Mole we had met someone who spoke to us about our impressions, because he was trying to encourage foreign tourists to come to Ghana. However, our understanding was that that Ghana was probably less attractive as a tourist destination than some other African countries. Most of the foreign visitors we had met were either volunteers taking time off, or else their parents coming out to see them, and exploring the country at the same time.

But as a place to live and work for a year and get the feel of Africa, it was pretty good.

Obrunni!

Chapter 7: Work and Play

Omega capacity building

The morning after our return to Gbawe Top Base we walked down to the office past the abandoned palace next to the recycling centre. We noticed a couple of burnt-out cars there, and asked Ken about them. He regaled us with a story that the ex-chief had returned to the palace and then been murdered. It seemed as if we had missed some excitement on our northern tour.

Having (more or less) successfully completed a round of feedback based on the test results obtained from Omega pupils, our focus shifted to trying to improve the procedures and build capacity within the organisation to make the best use of the time and energy spent creating, designing, taking and marking these tests. There were multiple areas where improvement was needed. One was the tests themselves, which often fell well short of ideal standards for quality assessment instruments.

Clearly, improvement was needed in data collection and tracking pupils through their career at school, so we could focus on areas where skills were improving or getting weaker. Pupil tracking could be tackled by assigning unique pupil identifiers which followed the pupils from year to year, but the problem was ensuring that teachers and others used these consistently. Unfortunately, usage continued to vary from school to school, and from year to year.

As well as helping me with these assessment issues, Sandie was kept busy reviewing the teaching materials which were given to the (largely untrained) teachers to guide them in their daily lessons. This was a fairly mammoth task, and involved her in frequent communication with the different subject experts.

I was spending time with Ato, showing him how the analysis worked, in the hope that he would be able to take over the system once I left – provided it was running in a reasonably coherent and straightforward fashion. At the end of April, Sandie ran a workshop for school managers on time management and report writing, with the aim of improving their management skills and help them to integrate the assessment reports into their oversight of the schools. She then went on a series of tours of the different schools, interviewing school managers about these issues.

Working in the office above Oblogo School had its trials. Frequently the power went off for long periods, though this was something we were

getting used to at home and at work. Some days when we arrived the office was locked, and we had to wait on the steps for someone with a key to arrive. The weather also turned rather stormy, with frequent tropical rain and thunder. On the 8th May I was in the office and Sandie was out, when there was an almighty crash from the end office, where the subject experts worked. Half of the ceiling had suddenly fallen down, and there was a terrible mess. Fortunately, nobody was hurt.

The great ceiling disaster

The next day we went to a conference centre near Weija Junction to run a test reviewing workshop with the subject experts, who write the tests. We tried to give them a set of criteria for assessing whether a test question was suitable or not, and then handed out short tests we had made up, to see if they could find all the problems, glitches and issues in the items we had put in. The results were interesting and generated some heated discussions. We also tried to insist that each test should be signed off by another member of staff before it 'went live', in order to try to prevent some of the worst examples getting to the students.

The next day was our last one in the office before returning to England for a short break. We had an assessment meeting, and as we were leaving we were stopped. I had 'Happy Birthday' sung to me, and we were prayed over and handed some gifts – a shirt for me and a dress for Sandie. So we said goodbye to Omega Schools for a couple of weeks.

Biriwa Beach

After returning from Kumasi and the north, we had a number of local outings at weekends, either to Accra or to Kokrobite Beach. The only slightly longer excursion was a stay at Biriwa Beach, along the coast in the direction of Cape Coast.

On 28th April we walked to Weija Junction and picked up a tro-tro to Kasoa. On the way it stopped and we were transferred to another tro-tro – probably because it was nearly empty. The traffic was bad in Kasoa and the driver did a short rat run through the dirt roads to join the main road slightly further up. In Kasoa we picked up a tro-tro heading for Cape Coast. We had to wait for it to fill up, and put up with a noisy evangelist who was haranguing the occupants through the door. It finally set off at 10.30, with us sitting together in the front. The journey was uneventful, and we were dropped off a bit before Cape Coast, at the Biriwa Beach Hotel.

We walked up the short drive and checked in. It was a really pleasant place, on a cliff above the beach with a pool and bar. Dumping our stuff, we went to the bar for lunch (drinks and pretty good sandwiches), sitting by the wall with a great view over the sea and the fishing boats Afterwards we changed and went down to the beach, which was deserted except for a few locals walking along it. We found a spot with a bit of shade and stayed there for a while, and then went for a walk to the far end. It was fascinating and scenic, with enormous waves crashing on to the rocks.

Biriwa Beach

We went back up to the hotel and sat by the pool for a bit, with the occasional swim. Later we moved to the bar for evening drinks, followed by dinner. The service was rather slow, and there seemed to be fewer guests around. The food was good – I had sautéed lobster and vegetables with chips, followed by a crepe with ice cream. We had a visit from the super-efficient German lady who runs the place. I think her presence explains why this resort was smarter and more efficient than others we visited. We took the remains of our bottle of wine back to the room, had coffee there and finished the wine later.

In the morning we spent time on the beach and at the pool, before checking out and going back to the main road to catch a tro-tro to Cape Coast. We walked through the town, and tried to get money out of an ATM, but with no success. We went to the Castle restaurant for lunch, and got seats by the window looking over the beach and the waves crashing spectacularly on the rocks. The food was good but unfortunately there was a long delay between bringing mine and Sandie's.

After getting a tro-tro back towards Accra, we stopped at Shoprite and did a load of shopping, but when we tried to pay for it with the Ecobank card it wouldn't work. We bought half of it with the cash we had left, and went outside where Alex came and picked us up. He took us to Ecobank, where we finally got some cash, and then back to Shoprite to finish the rest of our shopping. When he took us home, we found the power was off. Despite this, we were able to relax with drinks on the terrace to celebrate another interesting weekend away.

Back to Blighty

On 10th May we flew back to England, and checked into the Travelodge in High Wycombe town centre. There were two main reasons for this trip: to avoid the Ghana 60-day rule, and celebrate my 65th birthday. This visit was a short but busy one, and included a number of excursions with Claire and her two sons, as well as visiting friends and going for walks – with lots of bluebells in evidence, so different from Ghana!

My Aunt Margie was in a nursing home in Glasgow, and we organised a day trip to visit her, taking along Claire and her elder son, Charlie. We flew

Aunt Margie and Charlie

from Luton to Glasgow, hired a car, and arrived at her nursing home in the morning. We were taken to an empty coffee lounge where we could chat to her without Charlie causing havoc.

After a break for lunch at a pub we knew nearby, we returned to the nursing home again to spend more time with my aunt. She was delighted to see us, especially her great-nephew Charlie. The flight back was uneventful, but Charlie was pretty manic despite having been awake all day.

On my birthday, Sandie and I walked part of the Thames Path from Henley to Marlow, and then had a meal in the evening at the House on the Bridge in Windsor, with Claire, her partner Raf, Andrew and his wife Ellie. The following day, we had lunch at the Boulters Lock Hotel with the same group, but including Charlie and our two granddaughters.

Marlow, and dinner at Windsor

That was the end of our brief return visit to the UK, and it was time to go back to Ghana to get on with what seemed like real life there. One annoying discovery we made was that the travel insurance we had booked to cover our time in Ghana had lapsed, because of us coming back to the UK. This seemed to us completely ridiculous.

Home Sweet Home

Before leaving Ghana, we had arranged that James could use our flat on his brief visits, especially as there was a spare room he could use and this would save him paying for hotels. The day after our return to the flat at Gbawe Top Base, there was a knock at the door. It was someone coming to fix up curtain rails in the spare room, where James was sleeping. While that was happening, we stayed there with him and discussed work-related issues, which was quite helpful. After the curtains were up, we walked down to the office together. Later in the day James headed off to the airport to fly to Lagos on one of his business trips.

We swiftly settled back into the routine of the only home we had. We were used to going out to buy water and assorted fruit and vegetables from the little shops and stalls all around. The regular power cuts had become an accepted part of life, and we had a plentiful supply of candles and head torches to deal with them.

We made sure each night (when there was power) to watch an episode of our favourite US series 'Lost' on Joy TV. We had discovered, purely by accident, that this series (one we had watched avidly before, in the UK and New Zealand) was running at 8 o'clock each evening – we switched the TV on early one evening and saw familiar characters. At other times we would watch DVDs on the laptop.

James returned from Lagos after a few days, and stayed with us for about two more weeks. During his time with us, we managed to get him addicted to 'Lost' as well, so all three of us would sit on the sofa to watch it. During this period a group of Swiss bankers, who sponsored Omega Schools, turned up and James introduced them to us.

The following day James brought two of these bankers (Reinhardt and Dieter) back to the flat and we all had drinks on the terrace. Next we all went out together in a van, driven by Ken's driver, into Accra. We got to Oxford Street and walked round to Ryan's Irish pub. More drinks and a meal were consumed there, and a pleasant time was had chatting together. Just before 10 pm we left, and the two Swiss got a taxi back to their hotel in Kasoa while we got one with James back home. I suspect that James was showing us off to the bankers to prove that he had clever and experienced people working with him – rather flattering, if that was the case!

Before he left Ghana, James insisted that I spend some time with him

going over the analysis and feedback system that I was developing. His thinking was that someone in the organisation should have a grasp of how it all worked, as I would be leaving and the staff I was training would not necessarily stay long-term. Events later on proved this was a reasonable suspicion.

Showing James the ropes

May/June in Ghana is the main rainy season, and during this time we had a lot of downpours. Some days it was so bad in the morning that we asked Alex to come and take us to the office. Even when the rain stopped, the roads and paths down the hill to Oblogo were so muddy and slippery that we had to take great care when walking. In the evening, the sound of the rain on the tin roof would almost drown out the TV, and at night it would sometimes wake us up.

On 1st June the electrical plug on the lead for the pump that drove our water supply fell apart. When I looked, it had been incorrectly wired, which explained the problem. I took the plug off the toaster to replace it, and later on picked up some spare plugs from a shop and replaced the one I had borrowed from the toaster. All of the electrical equipment seemed to come from China, and was frequently sub-standard. The electrical sockets in the dining room began to fail, which meant that everything there, including the pump, was running off one working socket through an extension lead. I bought some replacement sockets and managed to replace the dodgy ones, so that we were able to dispense with the extension lead. A little bit of DIY is handy in Ghana!

During this period (May and June) we made just one trip to Accra, on Saturday 26th May. After lunch, we walked down the hill the other way from usual, ending up in Gbawe. We got a tro-tro to Hallam Junction and another to the Accra Mall. We went to the cinema there and saw a Tim Burton film 'Dark Shadows'. After that we looked round the shops and had a meal at the Rhapsody restaurant, which made a pleasant change. After getting some supplies from the Shoprite supermarket there, we got Alex to come and take us home.

On with the good work

Meanwhile, down at the Omega office, work on the assessment feedback system was progressing. In our absence more data had trickled in which needed to be added to the database I was building up. As part of the drive to develop unique student IDs, we had asked each school to provide class lists for their pupils, and these needed to be entered into the system and the names sorted out.

Dealing with variable student names was time consuming and prone to error, as well as giving rise to many cases of students occurring twice in the database. I developed some sophisticated matching algorithms to try to cope with these problems, but they were by no means foolproof. Once the initial input of class lists was done, they had to be printed and returned to the schools, so that the teachers could check them, correct inaccuracies and add students who had been omitted.

At this time I was also involved with interviewing a couple of candidates for statistical assistant, to help with doing the analysis of assessment data and producing feedback. Nobody new joined us at this point, so I began training Ato and James Dixon (transferred from another part of the office) in the mysteries of the assessment and feedback system.

By 13th June I had finished the initial set-up of the class lists, so Ato went off to Asempa Down school to print them. There was a problem with these, however, so the next day they all had to be redone. But we had no power and no cartridge for the printer in the office. Eventually, a new cartridge was acquired, and a generator and Heath Robinson arrangement of wires was rigged up, so I could now print them again. After that they were despatched to schools to be checked.

On 22nd June we had a team of data entry people with laptops ready to enter the results of the mid-term tests, and I began entering the first batch myself. A few days later there was enough data entered for me to ask my two trainees to start generating feedback. Scanned data also arrived, so I spent some time on sorting this out on our last day before the organisation moved to a new office in Kasoa.

A weekend at Kokrobite Garden

We also had two Sunday trips to Kokrobite Beach, which followed our standard pattern: tro-tro and shared taxi to the village, time on the beach, lunch at Big Milly's or Kokrobite Garden, cocktails in the upstairs bar at Big Milly's, and back the way we came.

However, on 23rd June we went on a Saturday and stayed overnight at Kokrobite Garden. Franco was in charge, because his wife had taken the kids to Spain. He showed us to our accommodation – a triangular chalet with a basic bathroom in the back. We dumped our stuff, changed into swimming gear, and headed for the beach. The weather was warm and sunny, and we found our usual shaded spot and stayed there for the afternoon. I ventured into the sea a couple of times, but it was filled with even more black plastic bags than usual.

A weekend at Kokrobite

At about 5 pm we went to Big Milly's and had cocktails in their upstairs terrace by the beach. Back at Kokrobite Garden we found a table in the outside area where there was a TV showing football, and sat there for the evening surrounded by other customers. We had drinks first – I had a very potent Cuba libre. Then we had the usual pizzas, with a bottle of chianti. After a couple of hours the power went off, but Franco put the generator on and everything continued. Although football is not my favourite thing to watch, it was quite fun sitting there in the evening surrounded by locals.

About 9.30 we went back to the cabin, but then the generator stopped soon after so we went to bed. The next morning we had breakfast, sat and read for a bit, then checked out and went to Big Milly's for lunch. The trip home was by way of a couple of taxis, and in the evening there was a massive thunderstorm – the first rain for a week.

A weekend at Akosombo

Apart from our regular weekend haunts, we made some longer excursions away from Gbawe Top Base, all within relatively easy reach of Accra. On 2nd June we decided to visit Akosombo, on the Volta Lake formed by the giant hydro-electric dam. As usual, the first challenge was to get to Accra. We set off about 8.50 and walked down to Gbawe, and picked up a tro-tro there as far as Kaneshie. From there we got another tro-tro to Tema bus station, and then walked round to Tudu bus station within the chaos that is Makola market.

There we boarded a tro-tro heading for Akosombo. After a wait it set off, going straight through Accra to the Mall, and then along the motorway. It ran into a lot of traffic, and the driver did a detour on dirt roads to get us heading north towards Akosombo. We eventually got out at Atimpoku, by the big bridge across the Volta River. We walked round to Aylo's Bay hotel, where we were staying, and got there at 1.20, 4½ hours after leaving home.

The sun was shining and the place is attractively laid out by the river, so we sat outside and ordered drinks and sandwiches while waiting for our room to be ready. The service was quite poor, and we were eating our sandwiches at about 2.30 when it began to rain. We moved to the main bar area to finish our lunch, and then were escorted with an umbrella to our room, a nice riverside chalet. We stayed there for a bit until the rain eased off, and at that point went and sat on one of the pontoons floating on the river to have drinks.

Then it began to rain heavily again, so we scuttled back to the room through the floods. We noticed that water was coming in under the door, but there wasn't much we could do about it. At 7 pm we went back to the main area, which has a tin roof so the rain was very loud. We had a leisurely meal with a bottle of wine, which it took ages for them to bring.

It stopped raining in the night, and in the morning there was a bit of sun early on. Breakfast was on the floating pontoon outside our chalet, and we chatted to a couple of young women who knew the area quite well. Afterwards we left our gear in the room and walked round to the Continental hotel next door to ask about boat trips. They said we could do one 'soon', but in the end we waited for about an hour for them to get the boat ready. While we were waiting a young local couple turned up as well, so we were able to share the cost.

Volta Lake and Dam

We set off about 10.15, by which time it had clouded over but was still dry. We sailed up as far as the dam and then back again, going under the bridge before returning to the dock. The trip took just over an hour and was interesting, despite the dull weather. Afterwards we returned to our hotel, packed up and checked out. We went to the road to get a tro-tro to Akosombo, but had to wait a while before one came along that was not completely full. We got off at the lorry park, and met a young German called Richard who shared a taxi with us up to the Volta Hotel, on a hill overlooking the dam. We had drinks and lunch there, which was pleasant and relaxing.

The plan was to walk round to the end of the dam and then on to a port which was supposed to lie up that way. We followed the road for two or three miles, but found nothing except views over the lake on the other side of the dam. We turned round and walked back to near the hotel, and were able to get a taxi back to the tro-tro park, where there was one leaving for Accra. This was quite cramped and uncomfortable, and the journey took two hours due to heavy traffic. Eventually we got out at the Accra Mall.

We went and had a drink at Rhapsody bar there, and did some shopping. We phoned Alex to pick us up, but due to a mix-up he ended up waiting in the wrong place. Eventually we found him and he took us home.

It may become apparent at this stage that travelling round Ghana without a private car is challenging, and requires patience and a certain amount of initiative. It can be extremely rewarding, however, and you meet some interesting and friendly people on the way. Also, driving in Ghana is not for the faint-hearted and I was happy not to have to do so.

A day at Aburi Botanical Gardens

On Saturday 9th June we decided to visit the Aburi Botanical Gardens, to the north-east of Accra. The trip began in the usual way: walk to Gbawe, tro-tro to Kaneshie and another to Tema bus station. The traffic was quite heavy, so it was about 10.15 when we got there. We found the tro-tro to Aburi and got in the front seats. While waiting I bought myself a new watch from a passing trader. The tro-tro left about 10.30 and headed north. There was some heavy traffic and a fairly rough stretch of road, and at the end a steep winding road to the top of the hills, with views over towards Accra. We reached Aburi about noon, and got out in the central tro-tro station.

We walked up to the botanical gardens and paid to go in – I had to pay 35 cedis to use the camcorder, which was a serious rip-off! We walked along an avenue of palms and went to a small restaurant by the guest house.

We had drinks, and cheese sandwiches and chips for lunch. We explored the gardens, which were a bit of a disappointment. There are a few interesting plants, but the area is not that large and it did not take long to see it all. The most fascinating thing was a wrecked helicopter, which made us feel like we were on a set for 'Lost' (along with a number of decaying buildings in the jungle). Having seen it all we went for a drink in the other (smarter) restaurant, before heading out of the gardens and back to the town.

Aburi Botanical Gardens

We got a taxi to take us back down the road a couple of miles to the Hillburi Hotel, which was supposed to have good views and a swimming pool. The pool was shut, but we saw the views though we had to pay 10 cedis to get in. We sat and had more drinks in their picturesque garden, and then took a shared taxi back to Aburi centre. There was a parents' day at the big girls' school, which meant the traffic was really bad. We got into a tro-tro heading for Accra (front seats again) and then it had to fight its way down through the traffic by the school. We had an otherwise uneventful journey back to Tema station, arriving at 5.45.

We walked round to the Osekan resort by the sea, arriving just as the sun was setting. We had drinks and a meal, though we ended up eating in the dark. Alex came and picked us up, and we got back just before 9 pm.

A weekend at Anamabo Beach Resort

The next weekend, 16th June, we did another trip westward to a beach resort. We walked down to Weija Junction and got a tro-tro to Kasoa, where we found the regular stop for going to Cape Coast. We just missed one tro-tro at 9.30, but got front row seats in the next one, although we had to hang about till 10.15 before it left. We drove uneventfully along the Cape Coast road, and got them to drop us off at the Anamabo Beach Resort just before 12.00. We checked in, and were taken round to our room, in a not very exciting beach hut in a compound.

Painted boat on the beach

We went round to the beachfront bar/restaurant for drinks and lunch, after which the weather brightened up and the sun came out. We went back to the room and changed, and spent about an hour on the beach. It clouded over again and got cooler, so we returned to the room, changed out of our swimming gear, and then went for a walk along the beach in the direction of the town. We passed a number of boats and came to a road leading through Anamabo town. There were a couple of events going on, with music etc, so it was not that easy to get through.

Ship-shaped posuban shrine

Finally we made our way to near the fort, and began looking for the advertised posuban shrines. We found one, which was not too exciting, and then wandered through the streets to find another couple. One was quite elaborate, built like a ship and well preserved. We headed back to the main road and went to look for the biggest shrine. When we Eventually got there it was quite tatty, and a man tried to charge us 10 cedis to take photos. We told him to get lost, went back to the main road, and walked back to the resort.

After drinks in the bar, we went for a walk eastwards along the beach. It was totally covered in rubbish, the worst we had seen. Back at the room. we discovered the hot water was not working. They arranged for us to move into the room next door, where the water was working. Sandie had a bath and I had a shower, although the shower rail collapsed in the process. The quality of the accommodation was quite poor, given the price they charged for the rooms. At 7 pm we changed and went back to the restaurant for dinner. It was windy and quite cool, and we tried to shelter behind some glass doors. The food was good and we had a decent bottle of wine.

It was raining the next morning, varying from light to fairly heavy. In a break we went to the restaurant for breakfast. This comprised omelettes and cold baked beans, with some fairly disorganised service. We returned to the room and read until 11 o'clock, waiting for the rain to stop. We decided to quit and checked out, by which time the rain had virtually stopped. Walking to the main road, we waited for a tro-tro, but eventually got a shared taxi into Cape Coast. There was a political rally on the way through the town, and we ended up at the Baobab café for a hot lunch.

Afterwards we went round to the square by the church and bought tickets for the Metro Mass bus. We piled on, and sat at the back. Then it appeared that we had to sit in our numbered seats, so we had to shift round. The bus finally left at 2.15 and headed back, through intermittent rain. We were dropped off at Shoprite at 4.30, and went in to stock up with supplies. Alex picked us up at 5 pm and drove us home – the road up the hill was worse than ever, due to the rain.

Togo or not Togo

By the end of June, we had been in Ghana for nine months (me) or eight months (Sandie), with three trips home. We were due to finish our year in September, but as we were only allowed to stay for 60 days at a time, that posed a problem. We had three options: apply for an extension to the 60-day limit; return to the UK again; or leave Ghana briefly for a neighbouring African country.

The first option was a possibility, but we had heard it was complicated, involving one or more trips into Accra and a lot of delay and hassle. We were not minded to fly home again, because of the expense and other complications involved. So in the end we chose the third option, with Togo as the obvious country to make for as a long weekend away. Working out the optimal date to go gave us the middle of July, less than 60 days from when we last arrived and also about another 60 days before we finally were going to leave.

Chapter 8: Changing Offices

New office, same challenges

At the beginning of July Omega Schools moved into a new office in Kasoa, a market town on the Coast Road several miles east of Weija Junction. For a start, this meant that we could no longer walk up and down to the office, as we were used to. The plan was for us to get a lift each day in the company van with a young man called John, who lived not far away from us. Then in the evening John would give us a lift back.

This plan worked well on occasions, but sometimes it was less effective. For example, we would arrive at the house in the morning to find that John had not brought the van back the night before, or was not going into the office that day. Then we would walk down to Weija Junction and catch a tro-tro to Kasoa. The problem with Kasoa was that there was a set of traffic lights there, and there was always a horrendous bottleneck of cars, vans and tro-tros trying to get through. Often we would get off a few hundred yards before the office and walk, arriving long before our transportation did.

This also led to problems getting home in the evening. If John was giving us a lift, then he would have to turn right to join the traffic outside the office, head west wait at the traffic lights, and then do a U-turn to go back east towards home. It would be 20 or 30 minutes later when he passed the office going in the right direction. We learned to wait till he did the U-turn and then cross the road so he could pick us up.

Other times, or if John was not going back to Gbawe Top Base, we would just get a tro-tro to Weija Junction and either walk home or get Alex to pick us up. One advantage of this option was that we could get Alex to stop at a shop and buy water, and he would carry it up to the flat for us – two big sacks of water balanced on his head.

The Omega office was a large and spacious area on the first floor of a modern building on the north side of the Coast Road. It was partitioned up into a number of cubicles separated by boards which came to head height when sitting at the desk. Sandie and I sat in separate areas – rather a change from our shared office in Oblogo. Eventually the place was equipped with wifi and a generator which came on automatically when the power went off. However, these enhancements took a while to be up and running, so initially we were little better off in that respect.

Welcome to the new office!

When we arrived there on our first day, 4th July, we found it a scene of chaos. There was no sign of the boxes we had packed up at Oblogo to be brought here, and a few days later we had to get John to detour to the office there to pick them up. That first day, I found a desk, but Sandie turned round and went back to work at home.

But after we finally got settled in, there were some advantages of the new location for us. We were very close to the heart of Kasoa, so it was easy to go out and buy things we needed, including fruit and vegetables from the market. Sandie and I used to stroll out each lunchtime and get the feel of the place, with all its crowds of people and vibrant energy. We would patronise the roadside stalls and buy fried yams or other food for our lunch.

The centralisation of all the Omega non-school staff in one place was also more convenient for us, as most people we were likely to need to talk to were now at hand, including the computer experts and the person organising the management database.

Friday at Newtimers

Another advantage became apparent on Friday evenings. We developed a habit of leaving work at 4.30 and walking over the road to the Newtimers Hotel, where we sat on their roof terrace and had drinks. We tried to persuade other members of staff to join us, but being highly religious and teetotal, most would not. Sometimes Ken and James (when around) would come over, but the only other regular attendee was Henry, the accountant. He was a local, but had spent some years in England, and was accustomed to the Friday night drinks ritual.

The main problem with the Newtimers was the incredibly loud sound system with a thumping bass, which even outdoors made it hard to hear each other. We asked them to turn it down several times, with no effect. On one famous occasion, when we were joined by a young lady from the USA who was visiting Omega, she just went over to the machine and turned it off. An illustration of the difference between diffident Brits and the American "go get 'em" spirit.

After drinks at Newtimers, we would walk along the Coast Road, possibly stopping at Shoprite to buy essentials and at Old Barrier to get cash from Ecobank. We would usually end up at the Sizzler for a meal, with my standard choice of lobster thermidor and chips, and get Alex to come and take us home.

Back in harness at the new site, my work continued with sorting out assessment data, matching it to class lists, and printing and collating feedback. In all this I was assisted by Ato and James D, who were beginning to gain in confidence at these tasks.

Studying the feedback

On Friday 13th July we had another teachers' meeting at the half-built church behind Shoprite. We handed out feedback for last set of mid-term tests, which revealed a number of issues which needed to be fixed. James and Ato ran some group sessions, which revealed a sad lack of understanding of how to interpret the feedback.

Way out West

On 30th June we set off on a long weekend into the west. Our plans included two more beach resorts, at Busua and Ankobra, with a visit to the apparent highlight of south-western Ghana, the Nzulezo stilt village.

We got a tro-tro to Old Barrier, and a second tro-tro to Kasoa. The traffic was pretty rough, but we finally got through and bought tickets for the long-distance tro-tro number 3 to Takoradi. We were the last on, and it left straight away, just before 10 o'clock. It was pretty cramped as far as Cape Coast, where a number of people got off and then there was more space. The weather was cloudy with a few showers on the way.

A few miles outside Takoradi the engine started making expensive noises, and then ground to a halt. After a certain amount of poking under the bonnet, the driver told us all to get out. He found another tro-tro (number 4) to take us into the city. A couple of blocks away we were directed to the tro-tro to Agona (number 5), which dropped us off at the roundabout with the road to Busua. From there we got a shared taxi, which detoured into the country to drop some people off, and then took us to Busua Inn. The guidebook map showed the distance as about a mile, but it is more like six or seven, so we were glad we decided not to walk. We arrived at 3.10, after seven hours, five tro-tros and a taxi.

At the inn we were greeted by their resident monkey and checked in (not by the monkey). Then down to their deck by the beach to have reviving drinks.

Busua: the monkey and the beach

The weather was cloudy but dry, with bouts of sun. We decided against the walk to Dixcove (reports of muggings) and instead went for a walk eastwards along the beach, having left most of our cash in the hotel safe. The beach was excellent, wide with good sand and stretched quite a long way. We followed a trio of bikini-clad German girls, who got me to take their photos halfway along. At the end we climbed some rocks, and got views of the waves and the sun going down on the beach.

Boats at Busua

On the way back we detoured through the Busua Beach Resort, which we'd considered staying at but decided against (very expensive). We had a nose round, and agreed it was all concrete and not worth the extra money. We walked back through the village to the inn, and then a short way westward on the beach to look at the fishing boats – quite picturesque. We went back to our room, showered and changed, before returning to the beachside decking for drinks and dinner. The food was OK but not outstanding, given the advertised French kitchen.

Dixcove

The next day it was cloudy with rain on and off all day. While we were sitting on the verandah outside our room, the monkey came up and stole my Sudoku pencil! We checked out about 9 am and got a taxi round to Dixcove. This was supposed to be picturesque, but was pretty squalid. We walked past the fishing boats and up to the fort, which was shut. We got a good view over the harbour, but then it began to rain. We sheltered in the doorway under an umbrella until it stopped.

Obrunni!

A shared taxi took us to Agona, and a tro-tro from there to Axim, further west up the coast. We looked at the fort there, which was shut as well, and had a brief stroll round the town. From there we got a taxi to the Ankobra Beach Resort, where we had booked in for two nights. This was quite pleasant, with thatched huts set amongst the palm trees. We went to our room (one of the cheapest) and then back to the restaurant for welcome drinks and lunch. There were occasional bouts of sunshine during lunch, but mostly it was grey. We went for a walk along the beach, but there was hardly any sand and it was covered in broken bits of wood and other rubbish, swept in by the rather wild sea.

We went back to our room and tried to sit on the verandah, but the door was locked and could not be opened. Then there was more rain, so we sat inside and read. I went to reception and complained, but the men who came could not open the door either. Finally, they shifted us to the bungalow opposite. By then it was quite late, so we had a shower and at 7 o'clock went round to the restaurant for dinner. It was quite a long walk, and the outside lights were not working, so it was just as well I brought a torch. We had drinks and a meal, followed by very weak cappuccinos.

The next morning, over breakfast, we met Rosemary, a German lady in her 70s who had lived in Ghana for 50 years, and who was coming with us to see the Nzulezo stilt village. At 8 o'clock we met up again to get the taxi, which drove for about an hour to get to Beyin, where the visitor centre was. We waited there to sign in and pay for our boat tour. We walked with the boatman and two others to the canal and got in the (rather leaky) canoe. The weather in the morning was quite good, with some sun and no rain. The boatman poled us along the canal while someone kept the leak at bay by bailing. We passed out from the canal into the wider wetland area, and then the boatman broke his pole and got a splinter in his hand.

From there on I helped the boatman to paddle, together with another man sitting in front. We reached the lake and headed for the stilt village which was our goal. After an hour in the canoe we disembarked and wandered through the village on the central wood and bamboo walkway. Apart from being on stilts in the water, it was a typical Ghana village –

scruffy with rubbish everywhere. At the end we reached the school and a place where we had to sign in again and make a donation.

Nzulezo

What we found strange was that there was little sign of the inhabitants of the village. We were told that Nzulezo had just been connected to mains electricity, and that most of the inhabitants were in their huts watching TV!

We returned to the canoe and paddled back. There were loads of canoes coming out and crowds of people waiting for a canoe when we got back. The taxi picked us up and took us back to the resort, arriving about 1.40. It was an interesting experience, but perhaps not as wonderful as the guidebook would have us believe.

On our return we went for lunch with Rosemary and her husband Robert, followed by a long chat. Afterwards we walked along by the beach, but it was still pretty wild. We went back to the room, but the power was off. We sat on the verandah and read. The power came on and then off again. I went and got a candle, and then the power came back. We had a shower at 6.30, and went to the restaurant at 7 pm. We had drinks, and food, followed by coffee and a cocktail (Ankobra sunrise). We were the last to leave at 9.30.

Beach encounters

The last morning of our western trip there was some sun, so we went to look at the beach again. We packed up and checked out, leaving about 9.30. Up at the main road, after waiting for about 10 minutes, we got a tro-tro heading for Takoradi. This took about 1½ hours, and the last part was slow getting through the traffic in the city. The tro-tro dropped us near the bus terminal, and we walked through to find out about buses.

We had seen a lot of smoke, and then suddenly people started running about and our eyes and faces began to sting. We realised we were in the middle of a riot, so quickly found a bus heading for Accra and climbed aboard. The journey took about 3½ hours, but was uneventful except for the excruciatingly bad and noisy Ghanaian soap they played on the TV. We were dropped off at Weija Junction and walked home, buying some bread and vegetables on the way.

The following weekend we had our usual excursions to Accra on the Saturday and to Kokrobite on Sunday, and after that it was time for our enforced (temporary) exile from Ghana to get round the 60-day rule.

A weekend in Togo

After a fair bit of agonising about how to deal with the Ghana 60-day rule, we had taken the advice to leave the country briefly and then return. The favoured place for this manoeuvre was Togo, a small French-speaking country on the eastern border of Ghana. So on 14th July, off we went. Alex took us to Tudu tro-tro station, which was heaving as usual, and we were grabbed by a little man and taken to a tro-tro heading for Aflao. The station abounds with these people, who for a small tip will take you to the bus you need – otherwise it can be a nightmare finding the right one. The tro-tro was quite smart and comfortable, and we piled aboard. It left at 9.15 and took 3½ hours. Aflao was very busy with buses and tro-tros coming and going. We changed some cedis to Togolese francs and walked along to the border.

We went through Ghanaian exit formalities, and then got entry visas to Togo with a minimum amount of fuss. The hassle began once we went out

Obrunni!

View from the hotel

of the border post, with people shouting and grabbing at us. Eventually we picked a taxi to take us to our hotel. It was no distance but there was an argument about the fare. We checked into the Ibis Lomé Centre, which is right on the seafront with smart grounds, a swimming pool and an outside restaurant. However, the place itself was a bit tired. We checked in and got a room on the fourth floor with a view of the sea. After dumping our stuff we went down to the bar, where we had drinks and massive cheese baguettes. The weather was dry with a lot of cloud and occasional sun, and quite windy.

We put all our valuables in a safe box, and – carefully ignored the warnings about it being dangerous around the hotel and on the beach – went out to explore. We walked east along the seafront as far as the Palm Beach Hotel, and went in to check out the bar and restaurant, which seemed OK. Then we wandered about, through the Grand Marché which consists of many streets full of stalls and shops, selling all sorts including a lot of clothing and dress materials.

Lomé city

We saw a couple of actual supermarkets as well, and came across the cathedral. This was quite impressive, with twin lattice spires painted brown.

We also found a travel agency and got a map of the city, and a list of possible tours to take the next, although we never did take any.

We walked back to the hotel, arriving about 5 o'clock. We had drinks by the pool, and at 7 o'clock we went down to the restaurant near the pool for dinner. It was quite breezy out there, and the food was poor and the red wine chilled. We went to the bar for coffee, but the air conditioning was so cold we sat outside on the terrace.

The next morning, Sunday, we got up and discovered it was pouring with rain. We went down for breakfast, and had tea and croissants. It was still raining, so we went back to the room to read and do Sudoku. At about 10.30 the rain stopped, so we went out to find the Ecobank and get more local cash. It was still dull and grey, but there was no more rain. We visited the Hotel Palm Beach for coffee (French-style cappuccino) on the way back to the Ibis.

We put the cash in the safe and went out again to explore the city. The police stopped us filming the Independence Monument. We did a circuit back through the city to the hotel, and decided we did not agree with the designation of Lomé as the 'Paris of West Africa'. At lunch they had no bread so we could not have cheese baguettes again; instead we got pastries from the shop in the foyer.

Then the weather got brighter, so we went and sat on loungers by the pool for a couple of hours. At 3.30 we went back to the room because the weather was getting greyer again, and there were showers. At 6 o'clock we went down and got a taxi round to the Palm Beach Hotel, and started with drinks in their bar, which had a pleasant atmosphere though it was extremely quiet. We went up to the restaurant, where we were the only customers and the food was so-so. Afterwards we got a taxi back to the Ibis at 8.30.

Obrunni!

On Monday we got up about 7 am, and went down for breakfast (tea and croissants again). The weather was beautiful that day – warm and sunny. After getting our bill we went up to the room to decide how much cash we needed, and then went out and walked to Ecobank again. We tried to get more cash out of the ATM, but it refused to let us. We went in the bank, and they tried to help, but after several attempts we had to give up. They would not even let us get cash out at the bank counter with our Ecobank card.

This particular shambles had long-lasting ramifications, because when we got back home and checked our online bank account, we discovered that two lots of cash that we had attempted to take out (and failed) had been taken from our account. We complained long and loud to Ecobank, by phone, email and in person, but the response we received was "We're looking into it" but no action. Eventually, months later, we discovered the money had been refunded to our account. At that point, joy was unconfined. Then, weeks later, the money was removed from the account again. When we protested and asked why, we were told they had evidence that we had actually received the cash! When we demanded to know what evidence, we got no response. In the end, we were forced to give up and write it off to experience, some years after the event.

Back at the hotel, I was able to get some cash out of the machine there with my Nationwide debit card. Then we finished packing up and checked out. We had enough francs left for a taxi back to the border. At the border we had no problems exiting Togo, and just had to fill in entry forms for Ghana. Then there was some hassle, and argument with the border staff, but eventually our passports were stamped with entry permits for another 60 days, which was the whole point of the exercise. Crossing back into Ghana made us feel as if we were returning to civilisation after a sojourn in darkest Africa!

We walked into Ghana and quickly found a tro-tro headed for Accra. It wasn't as smart or comfortable as the one we had coming out, but it did the job. Just before the Volta River we were hauled out by Immigration and our passports checked again, which was a bit scary, but they let us go on. We were dropped off at the Accra Mall about 1.30. From there we got another tro-tro to Mallam Junction, and then one up to Weija Junction. We walked home, getting bread and a pineapple on the way.

We agreed that it was a very moot point whether our excursion to Togo was worthwhile, compared with the hassle and expense of returning to the UK!

Back to work

We were now legally in the country until the end of our stay, in mid-September. Returning to the Kasoa office, I first had a session with James about assessment issues, and then a meeting of his newly-created Education Management Group, including myself and Sandie. There was discussion of where everyone would sit in the new office, and I did a floor plan to help. After that, I spent my time correcting bugs in the feedback and reprinting it.

A few days later we were both driven to Akorley school for the Choral Festival, which had been named in our honour. This was a particularly ironic tribute as neither of us can sing a note! We were given front row seats, and watched as choirs from each school performed on a stage. There were also a couple of dance events, and the programme seemed very long. As it happened, none of the performances lasted as long as advertised.

The Ian and Sandie Schagen Choral Festival

At the end we had to present the prize to the winning team, and then we were ushered into the manager's office for food and drink. As the food was meat pies and the drink was Guinness Malta (a disgusting non-alcoholic concoction), we made an excuse and got a lift back with Ken.

The following week Sandie began going round the schools to give the school managers their feedback. The level of enthusiasm and understanding varied widely, but she persevered with her task. At the same time I was developing Excel macros to automate the production of feedback in the future. The hope was that this would make the system more automatic, less labour-intensive, and easier for others to run in my absence.

I was working on producing anonymised versions of the feedback, in order to demonstrate our system to sponsors, both actual and potential. This was non-trivial, as it was necessary to make up student names to replace the actual ones on the feedback. Another task at this time was to match our ongoing assessment database to the newly-developed school management database. Again this was a bit of a challenge, as the two systems operated in quite different ways, with different software. Once again, we ran into problems with the variability in Ghanaian children's names!

Back home

After our return from Togo, life at home returned to its normal pattern. The main issue at the flat was that the airbed, which we used on top of the regular mattress to give us a more comfortable sleep, sprang a leak. Finally, we had to give up on using it, because by the end of the night it was almost totally deflated. For the remaining couple of months we had to put up with our hard Ghanaian mattress.

On 21st July we decided to go down to Gbawe for a change on Saturday night. On the way down the hill I slipped over, banged my knee and ripped a hole in my trousers. We pressed on, and walked through Gbawe and Mallam to the main road, which we walked along as far as Lloyd's Plaza, aiming to have a meal there. We got drinks and ordered pizzas, and were told they would take an hour. In the end they actually took an hour and 35 minutes, and arrived just before 8.30, when Alex came to take us home, so we had them put in boxes to take away. The pizzas were extremely spicy and not very nice, and packed in the boxes upside down so they stuck to the cardboard. Not a successful evening! The following day we had our usual Sunday trip to Kokrobite, which was rather more enjoyable.

Winneba weekend

On 28th July we spent the weekend at Winneba, a town to the west of Kasoa. We walked down the hill to Weija Junction – it was quite grey and miserable, with some spots of rain – and took a tro-tro to Kasoa. Just past the lights there was a desk selling tickets to Winneba. We got in the tro-tro, and after a while it left, and took us to the lorry park in the town.

We wandered around a bit, and eventually found our way to the University of Education southern campus, and through that down to the Lagoon Lodge, where we had booked in for the night. The place itself was quite smart, and our room was OK, but the bar was totally enclosed, rather than overlooking the lagoon as advertised in the guidebook.

Winneba

We had lunch there, and afterwards we went out again and followed a path down to the beach. This emerged next to a derelict beach resort, and there were plenty of locals on the beach and in the water. The weather had improved by then, and the sun came out. We walked along the beach towards the town, passing some picturesque red rocks. In order to avoid a section of beach which was in use as a toilet, we cut back towards the town. We discovered the old European cemetery, with a local 'royal' cemetery opposite, and then walked round to see the fishing harbour with dozens of boats.

On the way back we detoured to see a weird modernistic tower, raised by some sect in honour of a bishop. Walking back to the lodge through the campus again, we passed another weird modernistic tower – there must be an epidemic of them in Winneba. We detoured to try to see the lagoon, but as far as we could tell it had all dried up.

Back at the lodge we had drinks in the bar (even without a view of the lagoon). We went in to change, but we just rinsed our feet as the shower was cold water only. Our real problems began when we went back to the bar to get a meal. There were other people out there getting food, and a noisy crowd in the indoor restaurant, but we had terrible trouble getting served. Finally, someone came and took our order, for starters and mains (soup and fish and chips for me; yam chips and veggies for Sandie). We also managed to get a bottle of red (Austrian) wine. Then we waited for our food.

Waiters came out with food for everyone else, but not for us. After more than an hour we caught a waiter and said "What about our food?", and they said "What food?" – our order had been completely forgotten. After a while they brought some yam chips, which we both ate, and later still they brought my fish and chips. As I was eating it, they brought my soup, but I told them to take it away. Later still they brought Sandie's main course. By the time we had finally eaten, it was quite late.

On Sunday morning we had breakfast outside, and the weather was cloudy and grey again. We packed up and checked out, and left about 8.45. We walked back through the town and found a taxi to take us up to Winneba Junction, on the main road. From there we got a shared taxi to Appam, on the coast a bit further west. We walked along the main street up to the little fort on a hill, with views over the fishing harbour. The fort was closed, and the place was infested with irritating little kids who kept hassling us, but we got some photos none the less.

We walked back to the tro-tro station, and got another shared taxi back to Winneba Junction, and from there a tro-tro to Kasoa. From the lights we headed north up the road, looking for the Ecobank, the Melcom store and a hotel we had seen previously. The ATM at Ecobank wasn't working, and Melcom was closed, but we found the hotel and went to their upstairs terrace for lunch. We ordered pizzas, and these took 45 minutes to come, but were fine otherwise. Afterwards we got a taxi back to the lights, and then a tro-tro to Weija Junction. We walked home, getting bread and some fruit and veggies on the way, returning home about 3 pm.

By the end of July I had been in Ghana for ten months, and we were starting to think about life afterwards – whatever that might involve.

We began to receive rumours of teachers telling their students the answers to the tests, even writing them on the board. In order to investigate this, I developed statistical algorithms to spot anomalous results which would indicate the possibility of cheating. For example, if the whole class does well on a test, with little variability in scores, that would be suspicious. A large number of test items where almost all students in a class gave the same answer would also be worth investigating – even more so, if the consistent answer was wrong. This would indicate that the teacher got the question wrong, and told this incorrect response to their class.

Running this analysis threw up a number of suspicious cases, including a couple of schools with several classes giving cause for concern. Based on this clear evidence, James and Ken visited these schools and give the teachers concerned a serious dressing down. Whether this had any effect on the incidence of cheating in the long term, I cannot say. However, the idea that the head office had a 'magical' means of detecting such cheating may have helped to curb it.

On 12th August we were taken over to Kokrobite school for the annual Omega Schools prize giving. Alex came for us at 1.30 and took us to Old Barrier, where we took a shared taxi through to Kokrobite. We walked round to the Omega school, and arrived about 2.10.

We then sat there in the front row seats waiting for something to happen. Finally, about 3.15, things kicked off with the choir singing. An MC took over, and then I got to stand up and deliver my speech (already written for me). Afterwards Sandie presented certificates to the graduating KG2 (six-year-olds) class, and then there were prizes for the best pupils in each class. The whole thing ground to a halt about 5.30. We had to go and sit in the school manager's office for a bit, but eventually we made our escape and went round to Kokrobite Garden, where we collapsed in a heap and ordered drinks. Later Ken and his wife Lisa joined us for a meal there, and gave us a lift home.

Omega Schools prize giving

Back at the office, I was spending most of my time matching the assessment and school management databases. The new office at Kasoa had a large roof terrace, and on 31st August there was a whole staff meeting up there. The main item of business was setting up a social committee, and in the spirit of this we went over to the Newtimers afterwards for our usual Friday evening drinks.

September began, our last month in Ghana, and on the 3rd I did a training session for the assessment team on measuring progress. I was also busy documenting all the details of the testing and feedback system so that my assistants, Ato and James D, could carry on after we left. I brought into the office the acrylic paintings I had done during our time in Ghana, and presented them to some of our colleagues. They seemed grateful, but perhaps they were just being polite!

Our time was drawing to a close, and we were mentally preparing ourselves to say goodbye to all the friends we had made at Omega Schools.

Home affairs

A few days into the month of August I began feeling unwell, achy and lacking energy, so stayed at home for a couple of days. After I recovered, Sandie came down with the same problem and had to take some time off.

During this time the President of Ghana died unexpectedly while in office, and there was some suggestion that there might be some political unrest as a result. In the event this did not happen, and the Vice-President took over smoothly. He made a nice speech, saying that this had not happened in their country before, so please would everyone bear with them while they sorted out exactly what to do! The funeral was on 10th August, which was declared to be a public holiday.

The next day we had a minor disaster, as the bottle of gas finally ran out. We had used it for our cooking since I first arrived, but unfortunately it did not quite see the year out. The empty gas bottle was still heavy and we were unsure about where to have it filled, so I rang Alex for help, and he said he would come over. When he arrived about 3.30, he announced there was a local shortage of gas, but he had heard there was some at Oboko, just off the main motorway past Mallam.

We drove there, and joined a long queue of people with gas bottles waiting to have them filled up. After about an hour we reached the front, and went in to have the gas bottle filled and weighed. Alex carried it back to the car, and discovered he had a flat tyre. He pumped it up, and we headed back. But in Mallam it went flat again, and he had to stop and change it. I finally got back home with the full bottle just before 6 pm.

The next day we discovered we had a problem with one of the taps in the bathroom. A plumber came, and said we needed a new tap, but it might be expensive. In the end I bought a tap in Kasoa the next day, and he came back to fix it. We hoped that was the last bit of home repairs required, and were fairly sure we would be handing the flat back in better shape than when we arrived. In the end Ken announced that Omega Schools would continue to rent the flat, for the benefit of future visitors.

Our landlady, Elizabeth, ran the House of David nursery school next door, and on 20th August they had a massive graduation ceremony, with kids parading about, demonstrating gymnastics, and accompanied by loud music.

Finally, on 1st September, we attended our first and last Ghanaian wedding. We were invited because the bride was one of the staff at Omega Schools. In the morning Sandie went out to our local hairdresser, called Personal Touch, to get her hair done. My barber, at the little shop called 'Lord's Anointed', gave me a thorough job as usual, though it took about half an hour.

I returned home and Sandie followed a little later. I had a shower, and then changed into my suit and tie (first time in Ghana). Alex drove us to the half-completed church behind Shoprite. The wedding invitation was for 11.30, but the pre-service warm-up was in full swing. The choir was belting out gospel songs and the assistant pastor was jumping about and bellowing into a mike. Eventually the bride turned up about noon, and the wedding proper started. There was an order of service, which listed a large number of events.

A Ghanaian wedding

The sermon was very long, followed by laying on of hands by about six ministers, and several hymns. The main service finished at 2.30, and then we just had 30 minutes for photos. After that was the 'reception', which was rushed through rather quickly. They cut the cake and 'popped the champagne' (bottles of fizzy non-alcoholic drink shaken up till the corks popped out), and we were given bottles of pop and boxes mainly filled with meat to eat. The whole thing finished about 4 o'clock. We summoned Alex to get us and were home by 5 o'clock. We noted that in England wedding services are short but receptions go on for ages – in Ghana it appears to be the other way round.

A play at the National Theatre

On 1st August we finally got to see a play at the National Theatre in Accra. We left at 4.45 and Alex took us into Accra. We got stuck in horrendous traffic and ended up at the National Theatre just after 6 o'clock.

We bought tickets from a little man by the main gate, who told us it started at 7 o'clock and lasted 1½ hours, so that is what we told Alex. We then headed for a place attached to the theatre which advertised itself as an 'international restaurant'. When we got in, they announced they did not do food, just drink. So we sat there for

The National Theatre

a bit – Sandie had a Star beer and I had two rounds of gin and Sprite.

At 6.45 we went round to the foyer, to be told the play began at 7.30. We killed time wandering round looking at the artwork, and then went and found central seats in the circle with good views. We had the place to ourselves, until another man wandered into the circle and a handful of people took seats in the stalls. Altogether there must have been an audience of about thirty in a place which would seat about a thousand. The auditorium and the foyer were very smart, and it was a shame it did not seem to get properly used.

The play itself was called "A Slave's Tale", and spanned about three hundred years of a family taken from Africa as slaves to America, and eventually going to England. Some of the acting and singing was good, but it was rather slow, and lacking atmosphere with such a small audience. We assumed there would be no interval, but at 8.30 there was a 15-minute break. The play finally ended at 9.15, and we went out and were picked up again by Alex.

Inside the theatre

He took us home via the back doubles, and we got back about 10.15. He said there had been a big fire somewhere which had knocked out the power, and when we got back the place was dark. We lit candles and made sandwiches, as we were starving by then.

Last visit to Cape Coast

On 18th August we did our last weekend excursion to Cape Coast. As usual, we walked down to Weija Junction, and got a tro-tro to Kasoa. Then we boarded a long-distance one to Cape Coast, but got off at Mankessim. This was a town we had passed through several times, but never stopped at – we decided this time to have a look round. We walked about and photographed the statues on the roundabout, which we had seen a number of times in passing.

Statues at Mankessim

The town's posuban shrine was up a side road from the roundabout. It was quite spectacular, with a large number of statues in three storeys, including a two-headed monster. We walked back to the tro-tro park, but were told to pick up tro-tros for Cape Coast back near the roundabout. We found one there which took us into Cape Coast, and we walked round to Prospect Lodge and checked in.

Last views of Cape Coast

It was after 2 pm by then, but we walked through the town to the Baobab restaurant for lunch. The service was dreadful, and it took nearly an hour to get our avocado sandwich/salad. We went down to the castle and looked round the gift shops, and bought a few souvenirs, before returning to the hotel, and chilling out for a bit there.

We walked down to the Oasis beach resort, and sat by the beach with drinks. It was very grey and miserable all day, and quite cool, but we stayed there with our drinks watching the waves breaking on the beach. From there we walked along to the Castle restaurant for dinner. There were not many people in there, but we had a nice bottle of Venetian Malbec. The service was fairy bad that evening, with our meals brought out at different times.

The next morning it had rained, and after the usual slow breakfast we took the bus home. We had become quite familiar with Cape Coast, and it was strange to think we were leaving for the last time.

A long weekend in the south-east

Our last major exploration of Ghana started on 24th August, taking in the south-eastern part of the country. We planned a three-night trip, taking in a beach camp at Ada Foah, on the mouth of the Volta River, then Ho, the main town of eastern Ghana, and finally Amedzofe in the hill country.

We were picked up by Alex and taken into Accra, to Tudu bus station, where we arrived at 9 o'clock. We quickly found a tro-tro for Ada Foah, which left at 9.30. The seat was not very comfortable, and in front of us was a woman with a box of chickens. At last, we had discovered where the term 'chicken bus' came from! We finally arrived at Ada Foah at 12.10, to be greeted with sunshine.

The guidebook had suggested the Manet Paradise hotel as a good place for lunch, but we walked through the village and found it was closed. We went instead to the Tsarley Korpey hotel, a very smart place on the banks of the Volta. It was surrounded by upmarket private residences which lined the shore. We had lunch on a platform over the river, with good views. The food was tasty but the service rather slow. Afterwards we had a boat trip down the river, with a boatman and a young guide. We saw the fishing village and the beach camps from the water, and then encountered the first of the ocean waves coming up the estuary.

Ada Foah and boat trip on the Volta

From the hotel we walked along parallel to the river, through the fishing village. This was very different from other villages we had seen, being mainly mud-walled huts with grass roofs, each in a little compound of woven palm leaf walls. After about 30 minutes we reached the Maranatha Estuary Beach Camp, where we checked in.

We were given a grass hut with the Italian flag on the door (every hut sported the flag of a different nation), and shown the toilet facilities, which were very basic and lacked anywhere to wash. But the sun was shining, so we changed into beach gear and walked along the estuary shore, through a couple of other deserted beach camps.

The beach camp and our hut

Each camp had its palm trees painted different colours – ours was red, yellow and green (Ghana flag), while the others were pink, yellow and green or blue and white. We cut across to the sea, where there was a lot of construction work going on, and then round the point and back to the estuary. When we got back we changed again and went to get drinks.

The sun was going down and it got rather windy. We returned to the hut, and at 7 o'clock went out again to get the dinner we had pre-ordered. We got a box of red wine and some water, and sipped that while we waited. After the meal, we sat out there with our drinks for a bit, before returning to the hut.

We slept quite well, lulled by the noise of the sea, and got up at 6.30. There was no way of washing or shaving, so we just got dressed and went out. We had ordered breakfast for 7.15, but most of it came at 8.10, and my omelette arrived at 8.20. Afterwards we packed up and checked out. This was quite a process as everything on the bill had to be written out by hand.

We left the camp at 8.50 and walked back through the fishing village and on to the tro-tro station. At this point it became apparent that getting from there to Ho was going to be difficult – along the lines of "if you want to get there, I wouldn't start from here!"

We found a tro-tro to the junction at Kasseh, which left after waiting for a bit. At Kasseh we asked for tro-tros to Ho, but again everyone looked baffled. This made us wonder, as Ho is

The fishing village the major town in eastern Ghana.

Finally, we got one to Sogakope, across the Volta. From there we were told to get a shared taxi to Adidome, where we picked up a tro-tro for Ho. This was crowded, especially when a family of four squeezed into the seat next to me. To add to the discomfort, the road was pretty rough.

Eventually we reached Ho, and got out near the Kekeli Hotel, in the grounds of the big Evangelical Presbyterian church. We checked in, dumped our rucksacks, and went out looking for food and drink. We walked up to the White House bar and had drinks but no food. After wandering about a bit we found a little place (Royal Farm) which did us a late lunch. Back at the hotel we showered and changed, before going out to wait for a taxi driver we had arranged to come and see us at 4.30, about driving us around the next day. We waited and he finally turned up about 5.15. We dickered for a bit and agreed a price for tomorrow – 250 cedis (about £80), which seemed quite expensive.

From our hotel in the south we walked north through Ho, looking for the Freedom Hotel for dinner. We walked for about 45 minutes and then found it, though it had changed its name to the Bob Coffie Hotel. We went in and had dinner up on the terrace. It was OK, though we were on our own and the fish I had was pretty bony. We had coffee and then got a taxi back to our hotel.

The next morning we got up at 6.40 and had breakfast in the hotel restaurant. Our driver (Ebenezer) turned up at 8.10, and asked if he could bring his brother along. We drove out of Ho and into the hills, eventually reaching Amedzofe up a winding road. At the tourist office we paid for guided walks to the waterfall and up the mountain, although our guide (Destiny) warned us that the path to the waterfall was steep and difficult.

We set off anyway, and the driver and his brother came too. The first part of the path was fine, but then it dived steeply downhill, with a rope to cling on to. The guide was very helpful in getting us down, and with his assistance we made it to the bottom. The waterfall was pretty spectacular, with a good flow of water. Then we had to get back up again, which was another struggle, but we made it with no broken bones. Apparently, we were the oldest tourists to have made it to the bottom and back!

We made it to the waterfall!

On top of Mt Gemi

Wli Falls

We then drove to the foot of Mount Gemi (second highest peak in Ghana), and the guide took us up the footpath to the top. We got some good views, though it was rather cloudy. We came down again and went to a local spot for some drinks, before saying goodbye to Destiny and heading off. We asked the driver to take us to Wli, and he drove at a furious pace to Hohoe and then on to Wli. The first hotel we tried was full, but we went on to the Wli Water Heights hotel which had a room for us. The place had pleasant grounds and helpful staff. We paid off the driver, who grumbled and wanted more, but finally left.

After dumping our stuff in the room, we went off to visit Wli Falls (the highest in West Africa). We walked to the visitor centre and paid admission, and were told we needed a guide, who was fairly unnecessary as the path was flat and straight, crossing nine bridges on the way to the foot of the falls. These were highly impressive, with a lot of water and a rainbow at the foot where the sun caught the spray. We walked back and studied the craft stalls, and bought an ethnic game for our granddaughters.

After drinks at the hotel, we cleaned up a bit, and sat out on the verandah. At about 6.45 we went through to the dining patio and waited for our pre-ordered dinner, which arrived at 7 o'clock as requested. We were all on our own there, so we had coffee and then went back to the room. There was thunder in the distance, and we had another early night.

In the morning, after a decent breakfast, we checked out and went to find a tro-tro to Hohoe. We boarded one which took us on a little tour of the local villages before reaching Hohoe. Once there we caught a tro-tro bound for Accra, with seats in the front. It took us south via the bridge over the Volta near Akosombo, reaching Accra Mall at 1.30. We went into the Chinese restaurant there for lunch. The food was good, the service speedy, and they even did cappuccinos!

We looked in the Game store, and got some teaspoons to replace our dwindling stock. Alex picked us up at 3.15, and we asked him to take us to see the fantasy coffin-makers in Teshie, on the coast road east of Accra. He misunderstood at first, but then turned round and took us there through the middle of Accra. The traffic was quite heavy, but we eventually found two of these places and admired the workmanship of these amazing coffins, shaped like eagles, cameras, insects, coke bottles and so forth.

Fantasy coffin making

The idea is that the shape of the coffin reflects the interests of the occupant in life – so a fisherman has a fish-shaped coffin, and so forth. From there Alex drove us back to the motorway, but this was very busy and clogged with traffic, and we did not get home till 6.45.

During August and September we made a couple of our usual Sunday trips to Kokrobite, but on 8th September we went back to Kokrobite Garden for another overnight stay. Despite the accommodation and plumbing, we had a pleasant stay and an enjoyable meal, and chatted to Franco about his family and their travels. The next day we went down to the beach once more. The weather was good, and the beach was crowded with the usual mixture: young white females in bikinis, young black men chatting them up, others playing football, sellers with stuff on their heads, black kids playing in the water, and rasta dudes in unlikely attire wandering about. We had farewell cocktails at Big Milly's upstairs terrace, and then it was time to leave.

Final farewells

On our last day, 14th September, we were summoned up to the roof at about 12.00 for a farewell do. There were some speeches, and nibblies, and real champagne that James had brought. When he offered it round most of the staff took some, not realising it was alcoholic and not the coloured water they call 'champagne'. Some of them seemed to get a bit merry, being unused to the real thing!

Farewell to Omega Schools

We were given a big sheet of card with lots of nice messages. At about 2.30 I handed over the laptop of power to Ato, with all the software and data to run the feedback system. Then we quit, after saying farewell to everyone and taking lots of photos.

We took our last tro-tro to Old Barrier, and Sandie went in the Ecobank branch to complain about the absence of a refund two months after the incident in Togo. We spent 40 minutes in there, but she made no progress. We rang Alex to take us home, for the last time. We went round to say goodbye to Elizabeth and give her a painting, and then finished packing and had a shower.

James turned up just after 5 o'clock, and we had final drinks on the balcony. He brought a van with a driver, so we loaded our four cases into the van and set off for the airport, via Gbawe and Mallam. There was a lot of traffic, but we got there about 7.15 and checked in fairly quickly. James took us across the road to an outdoor restaurant, which was quite pleasant and atmospheric. We met up with Fatima and Caitlin, two of the Omega board members, and had drinks and a meal (red red for the last time). At 8.30 we returned to the airport and queued up for immigration and security.

We had a bit of a scare when an official came and pulled us out of the line, as we thought we were in trouble again, like the first time we left. But the man just took us to the front of the queue and said "In Ghana we respect old people, and don't expect you to wait in line". We thanked him, but had mixed feelings about whether we should be flattered or offended! At the other side we got some (expensive) cappuccinos.

The plane boarded and took off on time, and the flight was fairly uneventful. I had a large woman next to me who overlapped her seat and kept elbowing me in the ribs, w

hich was a trial. The food, wine and brandy were good, however, and I got a little bit of sleep, before the culture shock of returning to England and wondering what to do with ourselves next.

Reflections

Despite the many challenges, we really enjoyed our time in Ghana. The people are lovely and the culture is fascinating. It was an unusual experience being an ethnic minority, although we were always treated with respect and courtesy – not true all the time for ethnic minorities in the UK. The people at Omega Schools were fun to work with, though perhaps not always totally dedicated to the job in hand.

Travelling around to different parts of the country was fascinating, although not without its challenges and excitements. It is not to be recommended to those who value 5-star luxury and ease of transportation, but our experiences were always safe and often amusing.

My main regret was that I did not feel that the systems I set up were likely to continue in the way I had hoped. Soon after we left, my acolyte Ato left Omega Schools for a lecturing job in Kumasi, and it seemed unlikely that anyone else would be able to carry on the work. I feel that we gained more from our year there than Omega Schools did.

Obrunni!

Paintings done in Ghana

Here are some of the paintings I did of local people while we were in Ghana (originals: acrylic on canvas).

Going to Church   Lady in Green Hat

Beach Boys

Obrunni!

Obrunni!

Appendix A: Omega Schools Feedback

Feedback for teachers

Teacher feedback 1

For teachers we produced three different reports, based purely on the children's test scores in each subject and not comparing their results to those from other schools. In the first report we showed the scores for each pupil in each subject, and whether they were significantly above (↑) or below (↓) the class average. Pupils above average in all three subjects were marked as 'needing extra challenge' (**EC**) and those below average in all three as 'needing extra help' (**EH**). Children who were above average in two subjects and below in the other were also identified (**?**), so that the reason for their poor results in the third subject could be explored.

Figure 1: Example of Teacher Feedback 1

Example	Pupil Scores	Primary 1	Page 1			
		Scores and Relative Performance				Code
Pupil	Number	English	Maths	Science	Notes	
Lewis	100409		9	11		0
Issabella Abachie	100394			16 ↑		0
Princess Addo	100395		5 ↓	13		0
Felix Adazu	100427	5 ↓	4 ↓	8 ↓	EH	1
Theresah Afid	100396		19 ↑	14		0
Frank Afrifa	100428			12		0
Osei Afriyie	100429	8	10	12		0
Sarah Agbeko	100397	9	12	12		0
Emefa Agbozo	100413		14	10 ↓		0
Mary Aguzane	100403	9	12	16 ↑		0
Agyie	100440	10	13	12		0
Princess Aidoo	100400		5 ↓	13		0
Bismark Akomaning	100432			15 ↑		0
Bright Amankwah	100430	11 ↑	17 ↑			0
Ophelia Ampong	100398	10	12	11		0
Wienifred Andam	100399		16 ↑	14		0
Crappati Andrews	100431		15 ↑			0
Jonathan Andrews	100460		9			0
Emmanuel Anobil K	100437	11 ↑	12	14		0
Solomon Antwi	100433	10	5 ↓	11		0
Isaac Adam	100434	8	9	13		0
Gabriel Arhinful	100435		14	15 ↑		0
Richmond Arhoh	100436	7	9	18 ↑		0
Sandra Asiamah	100401			14		0
Ebenezer Asomaning	100408	9	15 ↑	14		0
Esther Attipo	100402			8 ↓		0
Ishmail Awudu	100459		13			0
Solomon Bansah	100409	9	8 ↓	14		0
Class average score		8.5	11.6	12.6		
Maximum score		18	25	25		

↓ means the pupil is definitely below the class average
↑ means the pupil is definitely above the class average
EH means the pupil is below average in all subjects, and may need extra help
EC means the pupil is above average in all subjects, and may need extra challenge
? means the pupil is above average in two subjects but below average in the third

133

Obrunni!

The explanatory text to help the teachers interpret this chart is shown below.

This table has six columns.

Column 1 lists all your pupils, in alphabetical order.

Column 2 has the unique number assigned to each pupil so their performance can be tracked throughout their time at Omega schools. This number should NEVER be changed by anyone.

Column 3 gives the score obtained by each pupil in the mid-term test for English:

- *Some pupils will have symbols beside their score to indicate that their performance was clearly above (↑) or below (↓) the average for your class.*

- *If there is no symbol, it means that the performance of that pupil was close to the class average, in statistical terms.*

- *At the foot of the column you will see the maximum score for the test, and the average score for your class.*

Columns 4 and 5 give the same information for mathematics and science respectively.

Column 6 identifies children with particular needs:

- *EH - needs extra help, because they are below average in all three subjects*

- *EC - needs extra challenge, because they are above average in all three subjects*

- *? - needs investigating, because they are above average in two subjects and below in the third.*

How this information can be used

It provides a clear record of the test scores obtained by each pupil, and their performance relative to the class average. You can use it to assess the strengths and weaknesses of individual pupils, and monitor their progress.

In particular, watch out for pupils identified as having particular needs:

EH – explain teaching points carefully for these children, and try to make sure that they have understood. Is there a particular reason why they are struggling, e.g. language difficulties?

EC – can you give these children extra (more challenging) work to do?

? – try to find out why the pupil is having problems with one particular subject. Do they find it boring or difficult? Can you try a different approach that may interest them more? Can they be given extra help in that subject, or encouraged to try harder?

Consult the Omega subject specialists for help in dealing with these pupils.

Teacher Feedback 2

In the second teacher report, we gave a table showing each child's results on each item – either correct (C), wrong (X), or wrong with a question mark (?). The last indication was based on a model predicting item results from total test score. If the pupil got a wrong answer when the model predicted they should have got it right, this was indicated with a question mark. The idea was that the teacher should explore why they got the unexpected result, and if there was a problem with their understanding of that particular aspect of the subject.

Figure A2: Example of Teacher Feedback 2

Example		Primary 1 English Question Responses		
C	means correct	blank	means the pupil did not answer the question	
x	means wrong	?	means unexpectedly wrong or low mark	
		(shaded) !	means all pupils got this question wrong	

Average class score: 8.5

Pupil	Total	Q1	Q2	Q3	Q4	Q5	Q6	Q7	Q8	Q9	Q10	Q11	Q12	Q13	Q14	Q15	Q16	Q17	Q18	Queries		
Max marks		1	1	1	1	1	1	1	1	1	1	1	1	1	1	1	1	1	1			
Felix Adonu	5	x	C	x	x	C	x	x	x	x	x	x	x	x	C	x	C	C	x		3	1
Osei Afriyie	8	C	x	x	C	C	C	x	x	C	x	x	C	C	x	x	C	x	x		1	3
Sarah Agbeko	9	?	C	x	C	C	x	x	x	C	x	x	C	x	C	x	C	C	C	1	3	1
Mary Agezane	9	C	x	x	x	C	C	x	x	C	x	x	C	x	C	x	C	C	C		1	3
Agyir	10	C	x	C	C	C	x	C	x	C	x	x	C	x	C	C	C	x	?	1	1	3
Bright Amankwah	11	C	x	x	C	x	x	x	x	C	x	x	C	C	C	C	C	C	C		1	3
Ophilia Ampong	10	C	C	x	x	C	x	x	x	C	x	x	C	C	C	C	C	x	C		1	1
Emmanuel Anobil	11	C	x	C	C	C	x	x	x	C	x	C	C	x	C	C	C	?	C	1	1	3
Solomon Antwi	10	C	x	x	x	C	C	x	x	C	x	x	C	x	C	C	C	C	C		1	3
Isaac Arhin	8	C	x	x	x	C	x	x	x	x	x	C	x	C	C	C	C	C			1	3
Richmond Artoh	7	x	C	C	x	C	x	x	C	x	x	x	x	C	x	C	x	C			3	1
Ebenezer Asomani	9	C	x	x	C	C	x	x	C	C	x	x	C	x	?	x	C	C	C	2	3	1
Solomon Bansah	9	C	x	C	x	C	C	x	C	x	x	C	C	?	x	?	C	C		2	1	3
Zaphinath Davies	11	C	C	x	x	C	x	x	x	C	x	x	C	C	C	C	C	C	C		1	1
Justice Fio	9	C	C	x	x	C	x	x	x	C	C	C	C	x	?	x	C	C	C	2	1	3
A Samuel Frimpo	11	C	x	x	C	C	C	x	x	?	x	x	C	C	C	C	C	C	C	1	1	3

The explanatory text to help the teachers interpret this chart is shown below.

These tables (one for each subject) show how each pupil scored on each individual test question. Find a pupil's name and look along the row to see how they performed.
Codes used are as follows:
C   means that the pupil gave the RIGHT answer
X   means that the pupil gave a WRONG answer
?   also means that the pupils gave a WRONG answer. But in this case it is surprising, because other pupils with a similar total score tended to get this question right.
blank   means that the pupil did not attempt the question.

A number in the Queries column indicates how many ? codes that pupil got. Most pupils will not have ? codes, so the column will be blank for them.

If a whole column has shading and exclamation marks, it means that all of your pupils got that question wrong, or did not answer it.

Obrunni!

How this information can be used

This information can be used in two ways, to inform your teaching of the class and individual pupils.

Individual pupils
- *Look along the ROWS to see how each pupil scored on each question. Can you spot weaknesses – topics where they may need help?*
- *Look at the ? codes. If a pupil who generally performed well did badly on one or two questions, why was this? Perhaps they were absent when the topic was taught. Investigate and see if the pupil needs additional support in that area, in order to reach their usual standard.*

The whole class
- *Look at the COLUMNS to see which questions, if any, your class as a whole found difficult.*
- *If there are any questions which ALL of your pupils got wrong, or failed to answer, why do you think that was? Perhaps you were you away when the topic was covered? Perhaps you could not spend enough time on it?*
- *Can you revisit the topic, and find a different way of explaining it to pupils?*

Teacher Feedback 3

The third teacher report showed the proportion of pupils in the class getting each item right, with a brief description of the item content. The intention was to give teachers an idea of which items, and hence areas of the curriculum, caused the most problems for their pupils and might require further work.

Figure A3: Example of Teacher Feedback 3

		Numbers of pupils			
Question	Description	Right	Wrong	Left out	Facility (% right)
Q1	What happens on "Saturday with Grandpa"?	25	8	0	76%
Q2	What do they wear while they clean?	10	23	0	30%
Q3	What does 'hurry' mean?	10	23	0	30%
Q4	What do they do at night?	17	16	0	52%
Q5	Picture 1 (arranging)	30	3	0	91%
Q6	Picture 2 (selling)	8	25	0	24%
Q7	Picture 3 (cutting)	2	31	0	6%
Q8	Picture 4 (giving)	1	32	0	3%
Q9	ant	25	8	0	76%
Q10	leaf	1	32	0	3%
Q11	cassava	5	28	0	15%
Q12	mouse	25	8	0	76%
Q13	is	17	16	0	52%
Q14	are	24	9	0	73%
Q15	are	15	18	0	45%
Q16	am	24	9	0	73%
Q17	is	20	13	0	61%
Q18	is	20	13	0	61%
	Exam as a whole				47%

Example — Primary 1 English Question Summary

The facility in the last column is the percentage of pupils who got the question right.

Questions with the highest facilities are the ones your pupils found easiest; questions with the lowest facilities are those they found hardest.

The explanatory text to help the teachers interpret this chart is shown below.

These tables, one for each subject, summarise the responses to each question for the class as a whole. The tables have six columns.

Column 1 Question number

Column 2 A brief description of the question

Column 3 The number of pupils in your class who gave the RIGHT answer

Column 4 The number of pupils in your class who gave the WRONG answer

Obrunni!

Column 5 The number of pupils in your class who did not answer the question

Column 6 Facility – the percentage of pupils who gave the right answer

Questions with the highest facilities are those that your pupils found easiest; those with the lowest facilities are those they found hardest.

How this information can be used

You can see clearly which questions, if any, your class found particularly difficult.

Why do you think that was?

Were you away when the topic was covered?   Were you not able to spend enough time on it?

Does the class need to go over the topic again? Can you find a different way of explaining it?

For the teachers, we deliberately did not give any comparisons between their students' results and those for other classes of schools, in an attempt to make them focus on improving the learning of their pupils, not compare their results with others'. However, for the school managers we felt it was important for them to see if there were strengths and weaknesses in particular classes or subjects, compared with Omega Schools overall.

Obrunni!

Feedback for School Managers

School Manager feedback 1

To produce feedback for school managers, we created 'Omega scores' for each subject, which were standardised to a mean of 50 and standard deviation of 10 across all pupils. Reports showing average Omega scores for each year group and subject, and comparing them with the overall average, enabled school managers to see how their results stacked up against other schools'.

Figure A4: Example of School Manager Feedback 1

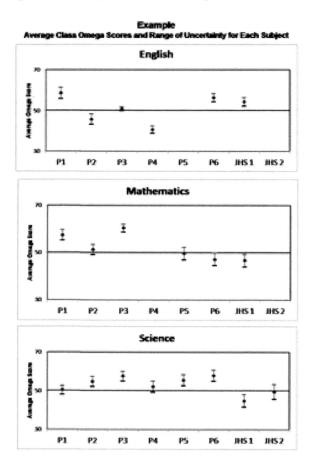

The explanatory text to help the school managers interpret these charts is shown below.

On this sheet there is a graph for each of the three core subjects. These make it possible to compare the overall performance of your pupils against the Omega average for each year group.

In each graph, the horizontal line across the middle represents the Omega average.   The vertical lines (one for each class, if data was received) represent the performance of your pupils.   The diamond shape in the middle of the line represents the average performance of each class.   But because there is measure of uncertainty with any test result, and because of the variation in the scores of individual pupils, statistical analysis shows that the 'true' average could lie anywhere between the top and the bottom of the vertical line.

*If a vertical line **crosses** the horizontal line, this means that the performance of that class is not clearly different from the Omega average. Otherwise, if the vertical line is above or below the horizontal line, then the class is definitely above or below the Omega average.   The distance from the horizontal line indicates how far above or below the Omega average the class is.*

How this information can be used

These graphs demonstrate which of the classes in your school would benefit from extra attention.

If the graphs indicate that one class in your school is positioned very differently from the others – if, for example, it is well below the Omega average, while all others are at or above – you will want to know why. There could be many possible reasons. For example:

- *Perhaps the teacher is new, or lacking in experience, or has been away due to illness.*

- *Perhaps several pupils in that class have only recently joined the school, and were not present for all of the relevant teaching.*

After investigating, you may decide that one or more teachers would benefit from extra support. If so, how could this best be provided?

- *Would s/he benefit from observing another teacher whose pupils appear to be more successful in the relevant subject(s)? This could be the subject teacher at your school, another class teacher, or even a teacher from a different school.*

- *Would a conversation with the relevant subject specialist be useful?*

- *Could additional training be given?*

Consult the subject specialist or the head of learning and teaching as appropriate.

School Manager feedback 2

We produced a kind of 'league table' plot of all schools' results in ascending order, with a large arrow pointing to each school manager's own school – this became known to us as the 'Hand of God' plot.

Obrunni!

Figure A5: Example of 'Hand of God' Plot

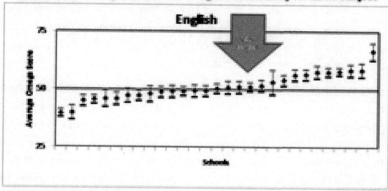
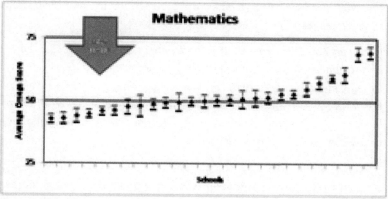
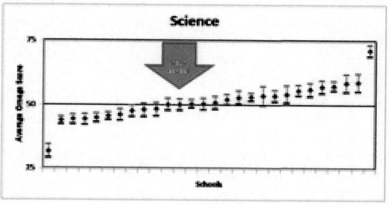

Obrunni!

The explanatory text to help the school managers interpret these charts is shown below.

The purpose of these graphs is not to compare year groups in your school, but to compare each class, in each subject, with the other Omega schools. You should therefore have a sheet for each class, with three graphs, one each for English, mathematics and science.

In each graph, the horizontal line across the middle represents the Omega average. The vertical lines (one for each school) represent the performance of the pupils in that school. The diamond shape in the middle of the line represents the average performance of the school. But because there is measure of uncertainty with any test result, and because of the variation in the scores of individual pupils, statistical analysis shows that the 'true' average could lie anywhere between the top and the bottom of the vertical line.

*If a vertical line **crosses** the horizontal line, this means that the performance of the school indicated is not clearly different from the Omega average. Otherwise, if the vertical line is above or below the horizontal line, then the school is definitely above or below the Omega average. The distance from the horizontal line indicates how far above or below the Omega average the school is.*

There can be up to 12[I1] Omega 'schools', as two [I2]schools have two streams which are analysed separately. However, on any graph there may be fewer, meaning that some schools did not provide all of the relevant data needed for analysis. The schools have been placed in rank order, with the lowest-scoring school on the left and the highest on the right. An arrow indicates which of the vertical lines represents your school, but other schools are not identified.

How this information can be used

As with the other feedback, these graphs highlight the strengths and weaknesses of the classes in your school. You can therefore use them to identify which classes or teachers may need extra support in one or more subjects.

Obrunni!

The additional information provided in this case concerns the rank ordering of Omega schools. It is not likely that any school will be consistently top (or bottom); on the contrary, you may find that your school ranked high for some year group/subjects, and low for others. Schools other than your own are not identified, but there is nothing to prevent you sharing information with other managers if you (and they) so wish.

It may be that you are concerned about the performance of one of your classes in a particular subject. You may notice that one of the schools seems to have an exceptionally strong performance in that area. You could discuss this with the subject specialist, who could identify the school, with the relevant manager's permission. If it was considered worthwhile, the teachers could meet to discuss strategies, and/or the teacher from your school could go to observe the other teacher at work, to gain ideas about effective teaching and learning methods.

Notes and comments

The limitation of this feedback will be immediately obvious. All of the scores computed were **relative**, and had to be, because we had no objective standard against which to measure pupils, classes or schools. Nevertheless, the feedback enabled school managers to see the strengths and weaknesses of particular classes in certain subjects, and (in theory at least) helped them identify teachers who needed support.

Use of feedback

Formative assessment needs two elements to work successfully: high-quality, relevant and timely feedback, and intelligent use by teachers to improve and focus their teaching. We believe the feedback we produced was both relevant and high quality – it was certainly more detailed and specific than anything we have seen elsewhere. It was as timely as we could make it, given that three stages were involved:

- Collecting the pupil scores from schools
- Analysing the data

- Printing and collating the feedback.

Data analysis was relatively quick, but collecting the scores from schools was a slow and surprisingly complicated process. Printing and collating the feedback also took time, as each individual teacher received a bound booklet containing all of the reports relevant to him/herself, as well as a simply worded explanation of what the tables meant, and how the information could be used to direct pupils' learning.

We did not rely entirely on written explanations. We ran training sessions for teachers, and for school managers, explaining the use and purpose of the feedback, and answering any questions they might have. Further, while the system was being developed, teachers and managers were interviewed and questioned about the usefulness of the feedback; some reports were dropped or modified on the basis of their comments. In general interviewees seemed pleased with the feedback and claimed that they found it helpful; but many struggled when asked to give specific examples of how it had been used.

Problems encountered

In operating the system, several problems were encountered, some of which have already been alluded to above.

- It was very hard to get data recorded and entered which was good enough to be used without a great deal of checking and recoding. Getting school staff to use consistent pupil identifiers was a nightmare, not helped by pupils' names being spelled differently each time, and often having first and second names transposed.
- It was emphasised many times (by ourselves, and by the senior managers of Omega Schools) that the purpose of the feedback was to **help** teachers to teach their classes, and individual pupils, more effectively. Nevertheless, many teachers remained convinced that the real purpose was to judge their work, and that they would be in trouble if their pupils did not obtain the highest scores. (As a result, there was some evidence of maladministration – I developed statistical methods of detection, but that is another story.)
- Before we left I trained staff in running the system we had set up, but unfortunately these all left shortly after. This highlights

146

another issue in developing countries – staff mobility, allied with a critical lack of suitably skilled personnel to operate sophisticated systems.

Ideas for the future

When we joined Omega Schools in 2011, there were only ten schools in the chain, but the number expanded rapidly. By spring 2014 (when I did some analysis for them from home) it had increased to nearly 40. Although a larger number of schools/pupils may enhance the value of the analysis, it becomes impracticable to run a system like that described above. The process of collecting data from schools, and producing feedback booklets, becomes far too cumbersome, expensive and time consuming.

Ultimately, I believe the only feasible way to get accurate and timely formative data in this environment is to maximise the use of IT: pupils need to do the assessments on screen, the data needs to be sent to head office electronically, and the results communicated to teachers and managers the same way. However, this would require a large investment in tablets or equivalent to allow all children to do the tests in a reasonable period of time. Given that, a high-quality electronic data collection, analysis and feedback system could be developed to provide formative information for teachers in such schools.

Printed in Great Britain
by Amazon

29807111R10086